FRANK LLOYD WRIGHT

The Complete 1925 "Wendingen" Series

FRANK LLOYD WRIGHT *et al.*

DOVER PUBLICATIONS, INC.

New York

Copyright © 1992 by Dover Publications, Inc.
Introduction © 1992 by Donald Hoffmann.
All rights reserved under Pan American and International Copyright Conventions.

Frank Lloyd Wright: The Complete 1925 "Wendingen" Series, first published by Dover Publications, Inc., in 1992, is an unabridged and uncorrected republication of the work originally published in 1925 by C. A. Mees, Santpoort, Holland, as *Frank Lloyd Wright: The Life-Work of the American Architect Frank Lloyd Wright with Contributions by Frank Lloyd Wright, an Introduction by Architect H. Th. Wijdeveld and Many Articles by Famous European Architects and American Writers.* The colophon of that edition further stated: "This book consists of seven special numbers of the art magazine *Wendingen.* It is edited and typografically [*sic*] arranged by H. Th. Wijdeveld (Amsterdam)[,] published by C. A. Mees (Santpoort) and printed by Joh: Enschedé en Zn: (Haarlem). Holland, April MCMXXVI." The contents page, originally appearing on page 163, has been moved to the frontmatter and translations of the articles by Robert Mallet-Stevens and Erich Mendelsohn have been prepared specially for the Dover edition by Stanley Appelbaum. The original text has been left untouched. The decorative border has been eliminated throughout.

Manufactured in the United States of America
Dover Publications, Inc., 31 East 2nd Street, Mineola, N.Y. 11501

Library of Congress Cataloging-in-Publication Data

Frank Lloyd Wright : the complete 1925 "Wendingen" series / Frank Lloyd Wright et al.
    p.   cm.
  Originally published: Wendingen. Santpoort, Holland : C. A. Mees, 1925. With new pref.
  ISBN 0-486-27254-0
  1. Wright, Frank Lloyd, 1867–1959—Themes, motives. 2. Wright, Frank Lloyd, 1867–1959—Criticism and interpretation. I. Wright, Frank Lloyd, 1867–1959. II. Complete 1925 "Wendingen" series. III. Wendingen.
NA737.W7F679 1992
720'.92—dc20
                92-31726
                CIP

INTRODUCTION TO THE DOVER EDITION

Frank Lloyd Wright was fifty-five years old and starting to feel his age when, toward the end of 1922, he confided to his mentor Louis H. Sullivan that he was utterly out of work. He soon left the Middle West and for a time established his studio in Los Angeles. His optimism ran deep, his imagination flourished, but his ideas rarely became buildings. In the five years previous to the *Wendingen*'s 1925 publication, in Holland, of *Frank Lloyd Wright: The Life-Work of the American Architect Frank Lloyd Wright,* he could in fact count three times as many unexecuted projects as realized buildings. The latter numbered only seven residences, all in the Los Angeles area, and two larger buildings in Japan. It was not a happy time for Wright, professionally or personally. The big book from Holland thus came to him as a wonderful encouragement, a fragrant bouquet indeed.

But that is not to say Wright had failed to attract significant attention in America. His early friend Robert C. Spencer, Jr. had published a thoughtful essay on "The Work of Frank Lloyd Wright" in the June 1900 issue of the *Architectural Review,* of Boston. The text was well informed, no doubt by Wright himself, and was surrounded by some seventy-five illustrations of buildings and designs, all representing a career that had not even arrived at full maturity. Still more illustrations—and of his first great buildings—appeared in the extraordinary March 1908 issue of the *Architectural Record,* of New York, wherein Wright chose to speak for himself. He was in the prime of life and his first "In the Cause of Architecture" manifesto proved to be as fine a statement as he was ever to make. Happily, it is reprinted in *The Life-Work;* a close reading can yield greater dividends than almost everything else that has been said about his architecture. Wright's unhesitant self-assertion must have angered countless American architects, just as the architects of the European vanguard tended to discount the idiosyncrasies of his architecture with a certain wariness expressed by several of the essayists in *The Life-Work.* Yet the great power of his work made a more indelible impression in Europe, especially through the publications of 1910 and 1911 by Ernst Wasmuth in Berlin. Thirty years later, the architect Mies van der Rohe looked back to that time:

> The work of this great master revealed an architectural world of unexpected force and clarity of language, and also a disconcerting richness of form. Here finally was a master-builder drawing upon the veritable fountainhead of architecture, who with true originality lifted his architectural creations into the light. Here, again, at last, genuine organic architecture flowered.
>
> The more deeply we studied Wright's creations, the greater became our admiration for his incomparable talent, for the boldness of his conceptions, and for his independence in thought and action. The dynamic impulse emanating from his work invigorated a whole generation. His influence was strongly felt even when it was not actually visible.
>
> After this first encounter, we followed the development of this rare man with eager hearts. We watched with astonishment the exuberant unfolding of the gifts of one who had been endowed by nature with the most splendid talents. In his undiminishing power he resembles a giant tree in a wide landscape, which, year after year, ever attains a more noble crown.[1]

Commonly known as the Wendingen book on Wright, because it was also published in seven issues of *Wendingen*

magazine, *Frank Lloyd Wright: The Life-Work of the American Architect Frank Lloyd Wright* in truth illustrates only twenty years from a career that spanned more than seventy. But what years they were! They began with Wright's first great prairie essay, the Willits house in Highland Park, Illinois, and went on to produce the Martin house in Buffalo, New York, the Unity Temple in Oak Park, Illinois, the Coonley house in Riverside, Illinois, the Robie house in Chicago, the architect's own home near Spring Green, Wisconsin, the Midway Gardens in Chicago, the Imperial Hotel in Tokyo and the Barnsdall house ("Hollyhock House") on Olive Hill in Los Angeles. As with Wright's manifesto of 1908, *The Life-Work* begins with the Larkin Building in Buffalo, New York—but with the floor plans first. The working drawings are crucial not because they display the central skylighted court, an old idea, but because the half-plans above the window sills show so clearly the vertical rifts, two-and-a-half-feet wide, that enable the stairway and air-supply towers to secede, visually, from the main block of the building. The vanguard European architects, better grounded than their American counterparts in architectural traditions and philosophy, were likewise more adept at discerning in such a detail of articulation the dynamics of a new architectural expression.

The pictorial emphasis in *The Life-Work,* however, is on buildings conceived after the Berlin publications of 1910 and 1911: the Midway Gardens of 1913–14, the Imperial Hotel of 1916–22 and the Olive Hill compound of 1916–21. Wright means to bring Europe almost up-to-date on what he has been doing. Oddly enough, in his third "In the Cause of Architecture" manifesto, written especially for the Wendingen book, he mentions the Larkin Building, Unity Temple and the Coonley house—all from the earlier years—and then jumps ahead to the Imperial Hotel and the Barnsdall compound, skipping all the rest. Because the pictures and plans are not keyed to the various essays, they seem to march through the book to their own rhythm. This easy informality distinguishes the Wendingen book. Another characteristic feature is that, although the book presents an international salute to Wright (much like a *Festschrift*), five of the contributions—counting the "Facts Regarding the Imperial Hotel" and the wholly nebulous afterword "To My European Co-Workers"—are from Wright himself.

The other essayists nevertheless compose a most impressive roster. Two of the contributors, notably, are senior to Wright: H. P. Berlage and Louis H. Sullivan both were born in 1856, or eleven years earlier. Sullivan's two papers on the Imperial Hotel have a certain poignancy. Published originally in the *Architectural Record,* they appeared in the last year of his life; he died in April 1924. In them, moreover, he acknowledged with great modesty and grace Wright's extraordinary romance of the cantilever principle of structure and his almost mystical sympathy for the nature of materials. Both were powers in which Sullivan did not share.

Hendrik Petrus Berlage, who lived until 1934, is often regarded as the father of modern Dutch architecture. He traveled to America in 1911 with the advice to seek out the buildings of Sullivan and Wright. The next year he lectured in Europe on what he had seen, and published his observations in the *Schweizerische Bauzeitung* (Swiss building journal). In contrast to so many American academics even today, Berlage found the work of Wright to be an absolutely independent architecture.

He also said the Larkin Building had no equal in Europe. Wright sent him a copy of his first "In the Cause of Architecture" manifesto and, in a cordial letter of November 1922, echoed the sentiments expressed more vehemently in his second "In the Cause of Architecture" essay:

I am not discouraged—but what encouragement I receive comes chiefly from Europe from men like yourself who have the benefit of a more cultured background, and from the younger men of my own country who begin restlessly to realize the emptiness of imitation—but who unfortunately turn too easily to a fresh model for imitation rather than to the *principles* that are eternal and forever fruitful.[2]

Wright's second essay has been interpreted as uncharitable or malicious, but it should be noted that the European contributors to the Wendingen book recognized the problem of superficial imitation and sympathized with Wright's denunciation of second-rate followers. Not many American architects, even among those who copied him, understood what Wright was about—a fact that greatly compromises the historical concept of a "prairie school" of architecture.

Jacobus Johannes Pieter Oud (1890–1963), much younger than Berlage, wrote about the Robie house in a 1918 issue of *de Stijl* (The Style) magazine, a rival to *Wendingen* (Turns, in the sense of New Directions). He, too, visited America and likewise failed to find Wright, who was in Japan; instead, he encountered Wright's mother. Oud is remembered for the graphic facade of his Café Unie in Rotterdam and his tightly disciplined housing and town-planning designs. His social emphasis is evident in the essay on Wright, with its concern for the universal rather than the individual and its conviction that the anonymous purity of Cubism, presumed more objective, can inspire a new species of classicism in architecture.

Robert Mallet-Stevens (1886–1945), a French architect and decorator, was a friend of Theo van Doesburg, the editor of *de Stijl.* Mallet-Stevens became very active in the 1920s. Four illustrations of his Paris studio appeared in the October 1928 issue of the *Architectural Record,* which also carried still another of Wright's continuing "In the Cause of Architecture" papers, this one addressing the potential of sheet metal, particularly copper.

Erich Mendelsohn (1887–1953), the German architect renowned for his tiny sketches of visionary buildings and for the bold plasticity of his Einstein Tower in Potsdam, had become a friend of H. Th. Wijdeveld's in 1919, the year after *Wendingen* was launched with Wijdeveld as editor. Mendelsohn attended a lecture by J. J. P. Oud in Stuttgart in 1923, and met Oud afterward. Having already lectured in Rotterdam, Mendelsohn knew of the tension between *de Stijl* and *Wendingen,* which he saw as the opposition of a cool and analytic objectivity to an emotional and romantic individualism. In 1924, Mendelsohn came to America on a lecture tour; urged by Wijdeveld, he called on Wright at his country home and studio in Wisconsin. Mendelsohn was greatly moved, as he wrote his wife Louise in two letters of November 1924:

I brought him the greetings of the whole of the young movement in Europe—to him, the father, the champion . . . .

We are at Taliesin, high up on the hill. It was a fantastic entry—into his house, to be his guest, the friend of this unbelievably rich imagination . . . .

It is imagination of an unheard-of richness—space, relationship with nature, details, materials, color—with masterly discipline. That is genius. It is the ecstasy of power in ordering space: a dazzling shower of sparks.[3]

Lewis Mumford, the American cultural historian and social critic, published his first book on architecture, *Sticks and Stones,* in 1924. He first met Mendelsohn late that year, and gave him a copy. Born in 1895, Mumford was the youngest of the contributors to the Wendingen book and the only one not an architect. Late in life, he recalled that he had little acquaintance with Wright's work when he wrote his Wendingen essay. Wright liked *Sticks and Stones* and quickly discerned Mumford's acuity and intellectual promise. He once said Mumford possessed a mind of Emersonian quality, a high compliment indeed. They first met in 1927, when he invited Mumford to lunch at the Plaza Hotel in New York. "One could not be in the presence of Wright for even half an hour without feeling the inner confidence bred by his genius," Mumford wrote in his memoirs.[4] In his later years, Mumford questioned the overpowering style of Wright's work and personality. But after Wright's death, he wrote Wijdeveld:

I thought of you at once, because I don't know of anyone else who was more like him in variety of skills, sparkling imagination and far-sightedness. It is as if nature, having produced Wright and in case he were to die at the height of his creative powers, had been anxious to create immediately afterwards in another part of the world a second Wright brimming with the same skills and all the signs of an individuality which is the result of environment, temperament and experience.[5]

Hendrikus Theodorus Wijdeveld, born in 1885, started work as an architect's office-boy at 12, and at 14 joined the studio of P. J. H. Cuypers, whose practice in the Netherlands was immensely successful. Wijdeveld considered himself the founder of *Wendingen* magazine, which began in January 1918, and he continued to edit it through 1926. In a 1921 issue he published Berlage's thoughts on Wright. As a propagandist, city planner, theater architect, park designer, typographer and bookbinder, Wijdeveld was also a visionary whose relation to Wright grew increasingly complex.

Four years after the *Wendingen* series on Wright's work, Wijdeveld was excited to hear that Wright had him in mind to direct a new school of architecture and the allied arts. Wijdeveld, too, had been planning an "International Guild," the patrons of which were to include Berlage, Mendelsohn, Mumford, Wright and even Le Corbusier. In April 1929 he wrote Wright:

It is a curious fact that great renewals often flash up on different places of the earth . . . at the same time . . . but independent of each other . . . Is it not strange that I myself am just now working out the same idea . . . . I want to erect an "International School of Architecture" in the surroundings of Amsterdam, but why not remove this idea, this work, to America, to the land with the nation of promise, to Wisconsin . . . to YOU?[6]

Wright had talked prematurely. When he first wrote Wijdeveld, much later, his proposal was much different. He wanted Wijdeveld to organize a European exhibition of his work. Wijdeveld obliged; the show opened in Amsterdam in May 1931. About a month earlier, Wright had further tantalized him by writing that a school of allied arts and industries, bolstered with a substantial endowment, was being formed in Chicago. He had suggested Wijdeveld as director, Wright said, at a salary of $10,000 a year, and with a ten-year contract. Wijdeveld found the offer overwhelming; he cabled Wright that he was ready to cross the Atlantic immediately. Wright had to put him off. Wijdeveld, perplexed, wrote Wright on June 10:

I made the exhibition of your work at Amsterdam (and through Europe) please, believe me, not for you, not for the sake of one man only, whom (certainly) I admire; but for the growth of an *Idea,* which might be now an *Ideal,* but which will one day be *Reality* . . . .

Later in 1931, Wright invited Wijdeveld to Wisconsin, where he said the school was to be started in a pilot project. Wijdeveld arrived at Taliesin in November. He at last met Wright, and they discussed what already was named the Taliesin Fellowship. Wright had prepared a three-year contract; a clause required Wijdeveld to invest $3000 in repairing the old Hillside Home School buildings, a sum that Wright somehow was supposed to match. Wright called his guest "Dutchy," embarrassingly enough. Wijdeveld returned to Holland, and the offer was withdrawn early in 1932. Wright wrote that the promise of the school was too fragile, that he would seek instead an American director. He in fact invited Mumford, who had no desire to give up his vocation as a writer. Wright and his wife finally launched the Fellowship in the fall of 1932; in March 1933, encouraged by its success, he once again tempted Wijdeveld with a position as director. Nothing ever worked out. Wijdeveld began his own small academy in the south of France in 1934, but it soon was destroyed by a forest fire.

In September 1945, after the deprivations of World War II, Wijdeveld again wrote Wright:

My wife and I are regaining our strength after we saw the edge of famine. We are still healthy and our spirit will rise again in a new and promising surrounding: maybe the "Taliesin Fellowship" is in full glow. Let me know . . . let us come, we two, to start the collaboration which broke-off at the moment the inflation broke-in and money lost its value. May 1931 become 1946! Fifteen years postponed and still full of hope. Still knowing that you are the world master-architect.

He wrote Wright again in October 1947:

The admiration for you lingered in me from the time I saw your work first, some 40 years ago. At that time I knew you as a prophet of a new era of culture and I followed your activities many years in silence . . . till it exploded at the time, when I founded the art-magazine *Wendingen* and published "The Life-Work of Frank Lloyd Wright," a book which you praised extremely . . . It was me who arranged exhibitions of your work all over Europe—Dear Wright—what has happened that you don't answer me in my days of distress?

Wright soon answered:

My dear Wijdeveld: You are one of the occasions that weigh on my conscience. I have not known just how to square myself with myself where you are concerned, so not knowing what to write I did not write.

But your frank request to come to the U.S.A. and join me deserves a frank answer.

You were right when, faced with a part in my enterprise (was it more than twenty years ago?) you said, "He is difficult to work with. It will take many years to build up this place. I have only ten thousand dollars. I do not know what to do." That was well said.

Since then many years have passed . . . . You were right in your conclusion that I would be difficult to work with. In fact I am impossible to work with . . . by any but one trained in and accustomed for many years to my way of work, that is to say. My disposition is that of a solo creative worker—even now, as you must know. So what outcome for a man of your wide attainments and boundless ambition but almost no experience in my way of work and life with me except one of frustration and eventual ill will?

Two rams in one small sheep pasture are certainly one too many. I would like to be of help to you and yours—your appreciation reached me when my fortunes were at low ebb and I am not ungrateful at this distance . . . .[7]

Wright invited Wijdeveld to be his guest at Taliesin; encouraged as well by Mumford, by Mendelsohn (who had come to America in 1941) and by the French painter Amédée Ozenfant, who conducted a school in New York City, Wijdeveld arrived here in April 1948. "I love to be here, in this vast country with its possibilities, its promising future," he wrote Wright on May 5. He visited Taliesin in May, then headed West, where he soon was invited to teach at the University of Southern California, in Los Angeles. Later, he taught at the University of North Carolina at Raleigh. After two years in America he returned to Holland.

The year 1925 seems not so long ago. Yet none of the contributors to the Wendingen book is alive today. Wright died in 1959, at 91. Wijdeveld, amazingly, lived into his hundred-second year, dying only in 1987. Mumford was in his ninety-fourth year when he died in 1990. They were the last; nevertheless, much of the buoyancy of their spirit survives in this book.

DONALD HOFFMANN

NOTES

1. Mies van der Rohe, "A Tribute to Frank Lloyd Wright," *College Art Journal* VI (Autumn 1946), pp. 41–42. The tribute was written in 1940 for a Museum of Modern Art catalogue that was never published.
2. Frank Lloyd Wright, *Letters to Architects,* ed. Bruce Brooks Pfeiffer (Fresno, Calif., 1984), pp. 54–55.
3. Eric Mendelsohn, *Letters of an Architect,* ed. Oskar Beyer (London, 1967), pp. 72, 74.
4. Lewis Mumford, *Sketches from Life* (New York, 1982), p. 432.
5. *Domus* (Milan), Sept. 1987, p. 10.
6. Wijdeveld's letters to Wright are on microfiche at the Getty Center for the History of Art and the Humanities, Santa Monica, Calif.
7. Wright, *Letters to Architects,* pp. 106–107.

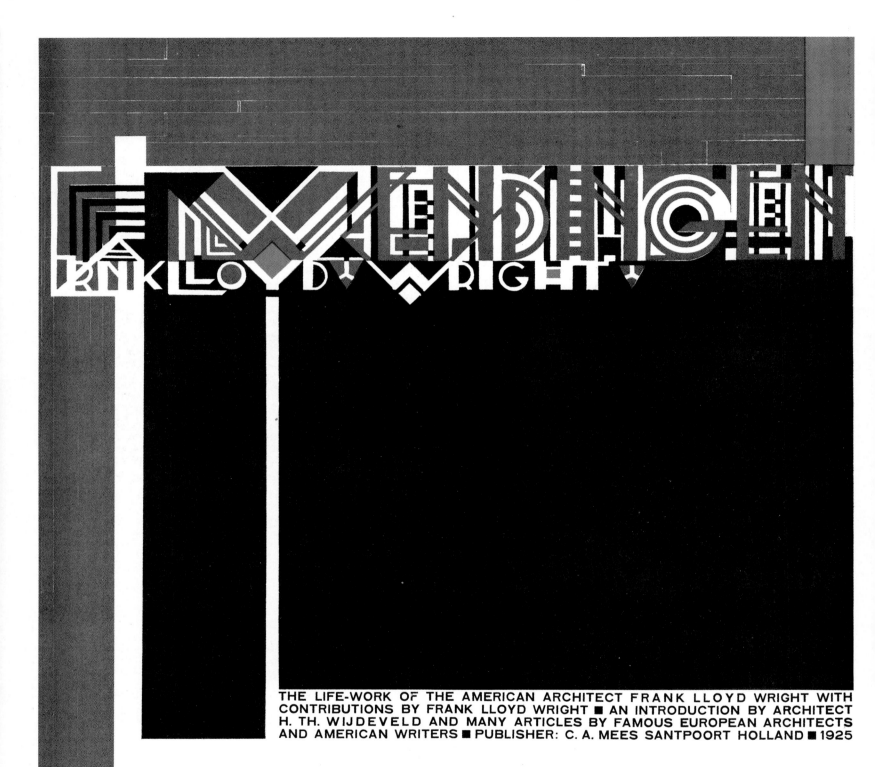

THE LIFE-WORK OF THE AMERICAN ARCHITECT FRANK LLOYD WRIGHT WITH CONTRIBUTIONS BY FRANK LLOYD WRIGHT ■ AN INTRODUCTION BY ARCHITECT H. TH. WIJDEVELD AND MANY ARTICLES BY FAMOUS EUROPEAN ARCHITECTS AND AMERICAN WRITERS ■ PUBLISHER: C. A. MEES SANTPOORT HOLLAND ■ 1925

[Original title page, reduced.]

CONTENTS

ILLUSTRATIONS   **CONTENTS**   ILLUSTRATIONS

ARTICLES

FRANK LLYOD WRIGHT BORN 1869
STUDENT IN CIVIL-ENGINEERING
UNIVERSITY OF WISCONSIN CLASS OF
1889 ■ WITH ADLER AND SULLIVAN
FOR SEVEN YEARS THERE AFTER ■
BEGAN TO PRACTICE ARCHITECTURE WITH
WINSLOW-HOME 1893 ■ LARKIN-BUILDING
1903 ■ UNIVERSITY-TEMPLE 1908 ■ COONLEY
HOUSE 1908 ■ TALIESIN 1911 ■ MIDWAY
GARDENS 1914 ■ IMPERIAL-HOTEL 1916

FRANK LLOYD WRIGHT

FOTO
NOV:
1923

SOME FLOWERS FOR ARCHITECT FRANK LLOYD WRIGHT

Out of the distance comes that which is near, out of rest comes that which is in motion. Trees rise up from the field, mountains from the valley. All is a picture of growth and unity. Eternally changing forms manifest the same wonderful secret of Nature, which exists in an interaction of all her elements. What is often taken for the power of the individual, arises rather from the impulse of the many, and what some few sowed does not shoot forth at the first sunbeam of appreciation. The new view of the world seems to enter upon a long Spring, which cannot pass into the Summer of general acceptance, owing to the ravaging gusts of the culture which is passing away. Those who lead the way must inevitably stand still and wait, for the masses who cannot follow are as much the burden, ... as the support. The solitude is too still and too barren to be traversed alone. What is a human life in this slow and wearisome movement, what is the labour of a single man? Nothing, ... because all is a picture of unity. All, ... because the picture is spoilt by the elimination of the smallest detail. Who supports is fortunate, who leads is the chosen one! Such a chosen one is the architect Frank Lloyd Wright.

From the silent borders of the prairies did he come to bring us the new architectural forms. He felt beforehand how this work was to commence and how to lay architecture gently in the bosom of this earth, along the undulating lines of the sloping fields was the most fruitful way of building, ... and fruitful it was indeed, for out of silence it grew into life. From the cottage, from the country-seat it was seen to proceed to the towns ... and unconsciously, as the surprising result of an unexpected force the sphere of his inner being passed to the factory, the school, and the commercial buildings. Thus the forms of his art grew and throug his influence, too, there came at length repose in architecture; for all life is seeking for a stiller background to the restless motion. Life is no longer turned inwards, it is turned outwards. The interior forces of the home are being supplanted by the exterior forces of the street. The new architecture will be the blank cinematographic screen which, quiet and tight itself, lets wild and swift life pass. Away! — all superfluous details. The new ornament is architecture itself, it is the shaping of spaces, the structure of the monolithic masses, it is the span of the plane, the rhythm of the details, the three-dimensional of the construction.

Although at the outset Wright felt unconsciously the extent of his task, the result is sure to be surprising... From the beginning his conscious strength lay in simplification; — because his earliest works already testified to a striving to ignore the dead "style"-ornament and this conviction he expressed in each new work with ever increasing seriousness. In the machine he saw the slave; — because he led the way in indicating the character of mechanical construction and considered the mass-product and the standard-type the greatest service of the machine. Normalization he knew to be his horizon; — because he saw dawning from afar the recognition of the subordination and insignificance of decorated details and regarded their arrangement, place and contrast only, as of value to modern architecture. His ornament is the three-dimensional; — because he creates architecture as a plastic whole and perceives the new spiritual forces working in the inner being of the masses, in the abstract form.

However, Wright's greatness is not his delight in the thousand atmospheres' pressure of the machine, nor his acceptance of the monotony of normalisation, neither the fact that he gives to the calculating engineer a place of honour in the world of the new architecture. Not in concrete does his greatness lie, nor in iron, nor yet in glass; not in the use of the new materials; but in the lofty attitude of his proportions, in the severe and stately rhythm of his walls, in the simplicity of his masses and through these in the proof that in all this renewing of material and form may lie a spiritual depth which promises the certain return of Beauty. For in the machine Wright sees poetic predictions, in concrete he shapes his architectural sonnets, his epic is the long expanse of the roof. He is like a teacher who opens for us a new world and gazes in admiration on the endless possibilities his "school" reveals to himself. His hard and rugged forms conceal a tender love of life, what he builds apparently cold and rugged, lies hidden in dreams and mingles with the many-hued plants and flowers with which he enriches the play of his forms. He is one of those prophets of the coming architecture who go forwards as it were in a trance and, untouched by the struggle, strike their master-strokes with never failing sureness, because they firmly believe in the poetical ground and ideal possibilities of the new architecture... of the civilization which is to come.

He is not to be restrained in his yearning after the realization of his dreams. Already in his drawings is conspicuous that which lends its snugness to the home, such a perfect command of form and colour, that for the sake of his melody-loving mind and for the satisfaction of his longings he runs ahead of the possibilities of execution, gives the rein to his fancy and creates ideal designs. And though he knows that America will not realize these designs, he soars up into the ideal and draws those splendid designs which need not be carried into execution... for, in coming into being they already give their creator such delight and offer so much real life, that for mankind they may sink into oblivion; to exist eternally for Wright himself. His drawings bear the mark of his love for his work and though he himself speaks of prosaic and plain contours, they are interwoven with mists and permeated with the eternal spirit of Hokusai and of the whole people of Japan. Yet they are never attempts to strive with Nature. No, he works as a phantast and creates his hazy tints which hover in horizontal bands and caress and aid and support the atmosphere of his art. All his work is directed to that on which his mind so fondly dwells: the realization of a new civilisation with an architecture of its own; which makes the machine its slave, which creates for mankind nobler longings, which brings repose from the prairie-borders to the heart of the desert, from the mountains down to the boundless main.

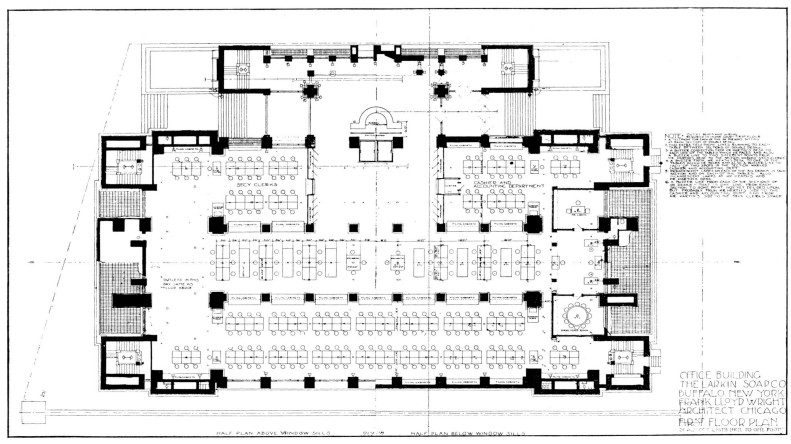

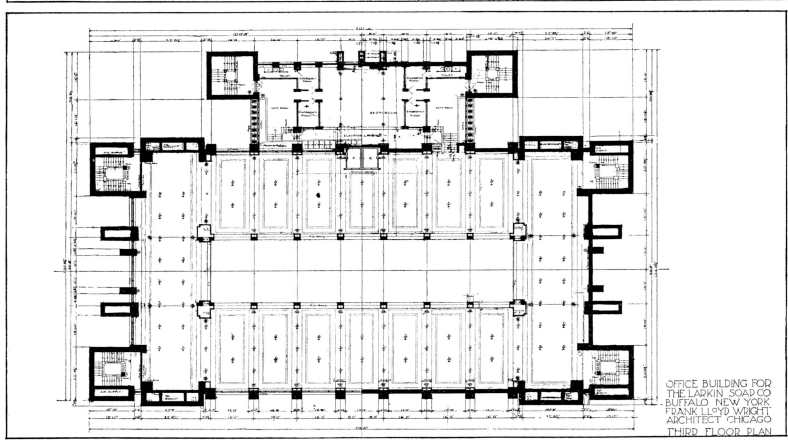

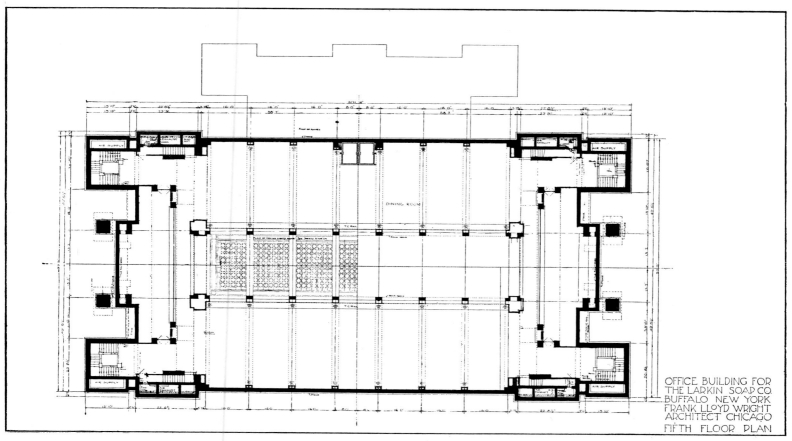

OFFICE BUILDING FOR
THE LARKIN SOAP CO.
BUFFALO NEW YORK
FRANK LLOYD WRIGHT
ARCHITECT CHICAGO
FIFTH FLOOR PLAN

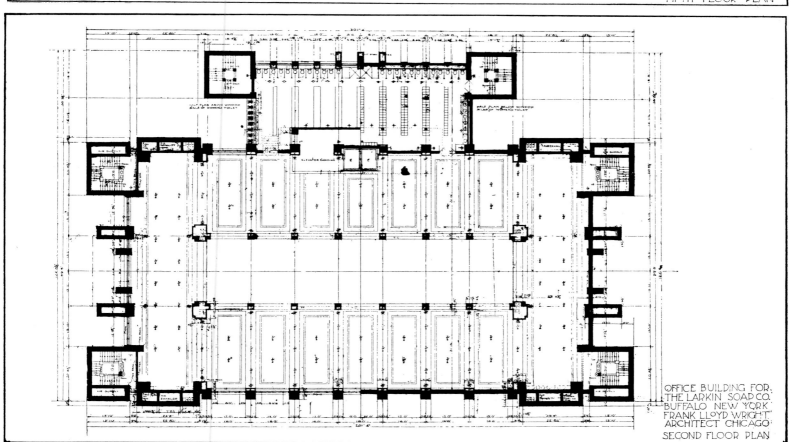

OFFICE BUILDING FOR
THE LARKIN SOAP CO.
BUFFALO NEW YORK
FRANK LLOYD WRIGHT
ARCHITECT CHICAGO
SECOND FLOOR PLAN

IN THE CAUSE OF ARCHITECTURE
□ □ BY FRANK LLOYD WRIGHT □ □

FIRST PAPER   MARCH 1908

Radical though it be, the work here illustrated is dedicated to a cause conservative in the best sense of the word. At no point does it involve denial of the elemental law and order inherent in great architecture. It is a declaration of love for the spirit of that law and order, a reverential recognition of the elements that made the ancient letter of great architecture in its time vital and beautiful.

Primarily, Nature furnished the materials out of which the architectural forms we know to-day have been developed, and, although for centuries our practice has been to turn from her, seeking inspiration in books adhering slavishly to dead formulae, her wealth of suggestion is inexhaustible; her riches greater than any man's desire. I know with what suspicion the man is regarded who refers matters of fine art back to Nature.

I know an ill-advised return is usually attempted, for Nature in external, obvious aspect is the usually accepted sense of the term and the nature that is reached. But given inherent vision there is no source so fertile, so suggestive, so helpful aesthetically to the architect as comprehension of natural forms. As Nature is never right for a picture so is she never right for the architect-that is, ready-made. Nevertheless, she has a practical school beneath her obvious forms in which a sense of proportion may be cultivated, where Vignola and Vitruvius fail. There he may develop the sense of reality that translated to his field in terms of his own work will lift him far above the realistic in his art; he will be inspired by sentiment that will never degenerate to sentimentality and learn to draw with surer hand the ever-perplexing line between the curious and the beautiful.

A sense of the organic in Nature is indispensable to an architect; where can he develop this sense so surely as in this school? A knowledge of the relation of form to function is at the root of his practice; where

can he find the pertinent object lessons Nature so readily furnishes? Where study the differentiations of form that go to determine character as he may study them in the trees? Or that sense of inevitableness characteristic of a work of art be quickened as it will be by intercourse with Nature in this sense?

Japanese art knows this school more intimately than any other people. In common use in their language are many words like the word „edaburi." Translated as near as may be, this means the formative arrangement of the branches of a tree. We have no such word in English. We are not civilized to think in such terms, but the architect must not only learn to think in such terms but to fashion his vocabulary for himself and furnish it in a comprehensive way with useful words as significant as this one.

For seven years it was my good fortune to be the understudy of a great teacher and a great architect, to my mind the greatest of his time-Mr. Louis H. Sullivan. Principles are not invented, they are evolved by no one man in no one age, but Mr. Sullivan's perception and practice of them amounted to a revelation at a time when they were commercially inexpedient and all but lost to sight in current work. The fine art sense of the profession was at that time practically dead; only glimmerings were perceptible in the work of Richardson and of Root.

As Adler and Sullivan had little time to design residences, the few that were unavoidable fell to my lot outside office hours. So largely, it remained for me to carry into the field of domestic architecture the battle they had begun in commercial building. During the early years of my own practice I found this lonesome work, sympathizers few and not found among the architects. I well remember how „the message" burned within me, how I longed for comradeship until I began to know the younger men and how welcome was Robert Spencer, and then Myron Hunt, and Dwight Perkins, Arthur Heun, George Dean and Hugh Garden. Inspiring days they were, I am sure, for us all. Of late we have been too busy to see one another often, but the „New School of the Middle West" is beginning to be talked

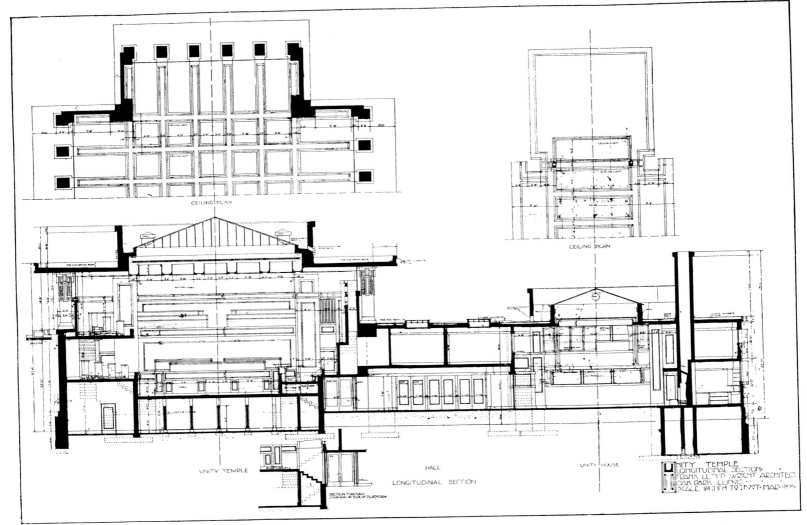

CEILING PLAN

CEILING PLAN

UNITY TEMPLE

HALL

UNITY HOUSE

LONGITUDINAL SECTION

SECTION THROUGH
STAIRWAY AT SIDE OF PLATFORM

UNITY TEMPLE
LONGITUDINAL SECTION.
FRANK LLOYD WRIGHT ARCHITECT
OAK PARK ILLINOIS
SCALE 1/4 INCH TO 1 FOOT MAR 1906

the sky lines of our domestic architecture were fantastic abortions, tortured by features that disrupted the distorted roof surfaces from which attenuated chimneys like lean fingers threatened the sky; the invariably tall interiors were cut up into box-like compartments, the more boxes the finer the house; and „Architecture" chiefly consisted in healing over the edges of the curious collection of holes that had to be cut in the walls for light and air and to permit the occupant to get in or out. These interiors were always slaughtered with the butt and slash of the old plinth and corner block trim, of dubious origin, and finally smothered with horrible millinery. That individuality in a building was possible to each home maker, or desirable, seemed at that time to rise to the dignity of an idea. Even cultured men and women care so little for the spiritual integrity of their environment; except in rare cases they are not touched, they simply do not care for the matter so long as their dwellings are fashionable or as good as those of their neighbors and keep them dry and warm. A structure has no more meaning to them aesthetically than has the stable to the horse, And this came to me in the early years as a definite discouragement. There are exceptions, and I found them chiefly among American men of business with unspoiled instincts and untainted ideals. A man of this type usually has the faculty of judging for himself. He has rather liked the „idea" and

much of the encouragement this work receives comes straight from him because the „common sense" of the thing appeals to him. While the „cultured" are still content with their small châteaux, Colonial wedding cakes, English affectations or French millinery, he prefers a poor thing, but his own. He errs on the side of character, at least, and when the test of time has tried his country's development architecturally, he will have contributed his quota, small enough tn the final outcome though it be; he will be regarded as a true conservator.

I have endeavored in this work to establish a harmonious relationship between ground plan and elevation of these buildings, considering the one as a solution and the other an expression of the conditions of a problem of which the whole is a project. I have tried to establish organic integrity to begin with, forming the basis for the subsequent working out of significant grammatical expression and making the whole, as nearly as I could, consistent.

What quality of style the buildings may possess is due to the artistry with which the conventionalization as a solution and an artistic expression of a specific problem within these limitations has been handled. The types are largely a matter of personal taste and may have much or little to do with the American architecture for which we hope.

From the beginning of my practice the question upper-most in my mind has been not „what style" but „what is style?" and it is my belief that the chief value of the work illustrated here will be found in the fact that if in the face of our present day conditions any given type may be treated independently and imbued with the quality of style, then a truly noble architecture is a definite possibility, so soon as Americans really demand it of the architects of the rising generation.

I do not believe we will again have the uniformity of type which has characterized the so-called great „styles". Conditions have changed; our ideal is Democracy, the highest possible expression of the individual as a unit not inconsistent with a harmonious whole. The average of human intelligence rises steadily, and as the individual unit grows more and more to be trusted we will have an architecture with richer variety in unity than has arisen before; but the forms must be born out of our changed conditions, they must be true forms, otherwise the best that tradition has to offer is inglorious mas-querade, devoid of vital significance or spiritual value. The trials of the early days were many and at this distance picturesque. Workmen seldom like to think, especially if there is financial risk entailed; at your peril do you disturb their established processes mental or technical. To do anything in an unusual, even if in a better and simpler way, is to complicate the situation at once. Simple things at that time in any industrial field were nowhere at hand. A piece of wood without a moulding was an anomaly; a plain wooden slat instead of a turned baluster a joke; the omission of the mer-chantable „grille" a crime; plain fabrics for hangings or floor covering were nowhere to be found in stock. To become the recognized enemy of the established industrial order was no light matter, for soon whenever a set of my drawings was presented to a Chicago mill-man for figures he would willingly enough unroll it, read the architect's name, shake his head and return it with the remark that he was „not hunting for trouble;" sagacious owners and general contractors tried cutting out the name, but in vain, the mill-man's perspicacity was rat-like, he had come to know „the look of the thing." So, in addition to the special preparation in any case necessary for every little matter of construction and finishing, special detail drawings were necessary merely to show the things to be left off or not done, and not only studied designs for every part had to be made but quantity surveys and schedules of mill work furnished the contractors beside. This, in a year or two, brought the architect face to face with the fact that the fee for his service „established" by the American Insti-tute of Architects was intended for something stock and shop, for it would not even pay for the bare drawings necessary for conscientious work.

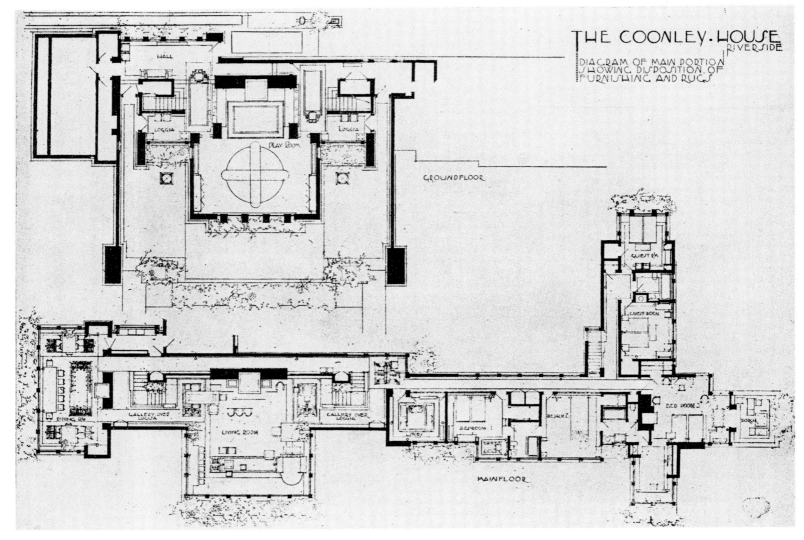

THE COONLEY·HOUSE
RIVERSIDE
DIAGRAM OF MAIN PORTION
SHOWING DISPOSITION OF
FURNISHING AND RUGS

The relation of the architect to the economic and industrial movement of his time, in any fine art sense, is still an affair so sadly out of joint that no one may easily reconcile it. All agree that something has gone wrong and except the architect be a plan factory magnate, who has reduced his art to a philosophy of old clothes and sells misfit or made-over-ready-to-wear garments with commercial aplomb and social distinction, he cannot succeed on the present basis established by common practice. In addition to a situation already complicated for them, a necessarily increased fee stared in the face of the clients who dared. Some did dare, as the illustrations prove.

The struggle then was and still is to make „good architecture," „good business." It is perhaps significant that in the beginning it was very difficult to secure a building loan on any terms upon one of these houses, now it is easy to secure a better loan than ordinary; but how far success has attended this ambition the owners of these buildings alone can testify. Their trials have heen many, but each, I think, feels that he has as much house for his money as his neighbors, with something in the home intrinsically valuable besides, which will not be out of fashion in one lifetime, and which contributes steadily to his dignity and his pleasure as an individual.

It would not be useful to dwell further upon difficulties encountered, for it is the common story of simple progression everywhere in any field; I merely wish to trace here the „motif" behind the types. A study of the illustrations will show that the buildings presented fall readily into three groups having a family resemblance; the low-pitched hip roofs, heaped together in pyramidal fashion, or presenting quiet, unbroken sky lines; the low roofs with simple pediments countering on long ridges; and those topped with a simple slab. Of the first type, the Winslow, Henderson, Willits, Thomas, Heurtley, Heath, Cheney, Martin, Little, Gridley, Millard, Tomek, Coonley and Westcott houses, the Hillside Home School and the Pettit Memorial Chapel are typical. Of the second type the Bradley, Hickox, Davenport and Dana houses are typical. Of the third, Atelier for Richard Bock, Unity Church, the concrete house of the Ladies' Home Journal and other designs in process of execution. The Larking Building is a simple, dignified utterance of a plain, utilitarian type with sheer brick walls and simple stone copings. The studio is merely an early experiment in „articulation."

Photographs do not adequately present these subjects. A building has a presence as has a person that defies the photographer, and the color so necessary to the complete expression of the form is necessarily lacking,

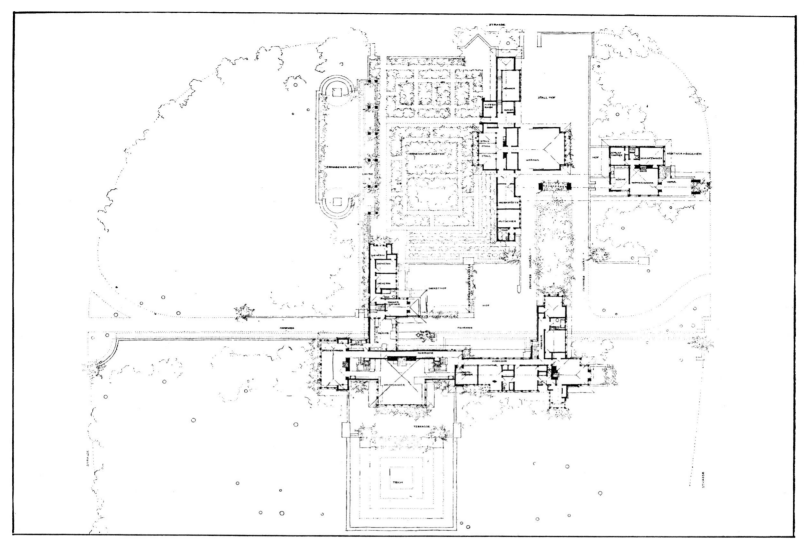

but it will be noticed that all the structures stand upon their foundations to the eye as well as physically. There is good, substantial preparation at the ground for all the buildings and it is the first grammatical expression of all the types. This preparation, or watertable, is to these buildings what the stylobate was to the ancient Greek temple. To gain it, it was necessary to reverse the established practice of setting the supports of the building to the outside of the wall and to set them to the inside, so as to leave the necessary support for the outer base. This was natural enough and good enough construction but many an owner was disturbed by private information from the practical contractor to the effect that he would have his whole house in the cellar if he submitted to it. This was at the time a marked innovation though the most natural thing in the world, and to me, to this day, indispensable.

With this innovation established, one horizontal stripe of raw material, the foundation wall above ground, was eliminated and the complete grammar of type one made possible. A simple, unbroken wall surface from foot to level of second story sill was thus secured, a change of material occurring at that point to form the simple frieze that characterizes the earlier buildings. Even this was frequently omitted as in the Francis apartments and many other buildings and the wall was let alone

from base to cornice or eaves. „Dress reform houses" they were called, I remember, by the charitably disposed. What others called them will hardly bear repetition. As the wall surfaces were thus simplified and emphasized the matter of fenestration became exceedingly difficult and more than ever important, and I gloated over the beautiful buildings I could build if only it were unnecessary to cut holes in them; but the holes were managed at first frankly as in the Winslow house and later as elementary constituents of the structure grouped in rhythmical fashion, so that all the light and air and prospect the most rabid client could wish would not be too much from an artistic standpoint; and of this achievement I am proud. The groups are managed, too, whenever required, so that overhanging eaves do not shade them, although the walls are still protected from the weather. Soon the poetry-crushing characteristics of the guillotine window, which was then firmly rooted, became apparent and, single-handed I waged a determined battle for casements swinging out, although it was necessary to have special hardware made for them as there was none to be had this side of England. Clients would come ready to accept any innovation but „those swinging windows," and when told that they were in the nature of the proposition and that they must take them or leave the rest, they frequently em-

ployed „the other fellow" to give them something „near," with the „practical" windows dear to their hearts.

With the grammar so far established, came an expression pure and simple, even classic in atmosphere, using that much-abused word in its best sense; implying, that is, a certain sweet reasonableness of form and outline naturally dignified.

I have observed that Nature usually perfects her forms; the individuality of the attribute is seldom sacrificed; that is, deformed or mutilated by co-operative parts. She rarely says a thing and tries to take it back at the same time. She would not sanction the „classic" proceeding of, say, establishing an „order," a collonade, then building walls between the columns of the order reducing them to pilasters, thereafter cutting holes in the wall and pasting on cornices with more pilasters around them, with the result that every form is outraged, the whole an abominable mutilation, as is most of the architecture of the Renaissance wherein style corrodes style and all the forms are stultified.

In laying out the ground plans for even the more insignificant of these buildings a simple axial law and order and the ordered spacing upon a system of certain structural units definitely established for each structure in accord with its scheme of practical construction and aesthetic proportion is practiced as an expedient to simplify the technical difficulties of execution, and, although the symmetry may not be obvious always the balance is usually maintained. The plans are as a rule much more articulate than is the school product of the Beaux Arts. The individuality of the various functions of the various features is more highly developed; all the forms are complete in themselves and frequently do duty at the same time from within and without as decorative attributes of the whole. This tendency to greater individuality of the parts emphasized by more and more complete articulation will be seen in the plans for Unity Church, the cottage for Elizabeth Stone at Glencoe and the Avery Coonley house in process of construction at Riverside, Illinois. These ground plans are merely the actual projection of a carefully considered whole. The „architecture" is not „thrown up" as an artistic exercise, a matter of elevation from a preconceived ground plan. The schemes are conceived in three dimensions as organic entities, let the picturesque perspective fall how it will. While a sense of the incidental perspectives the design will develop is always present, I have great faith that if the thing is rightly put together in true organic sense with proportions actually right the picturesque will take care of itself. No man

ever built a building worthy the name of architecture who fashioned it in perspective sketch to his taste and then fudged the plan to suit. Such methods produce mere scene-painting. A perspective may be a proof but it is no nurture.

As to the mass values of the buildings the aesthetic principles outlined in proposition III will account in a measure for their character.

In the matter of decoration the tendency has been to indulge in it less and less, merely providing certain architectural preparation for natural foliage or flowers, as it is managed in say, the entrance to the Lawrence house at Springfield. This use of natural foliage and flowers for decoration is carried to quite an extent in all the designs and, although the buildings are complete without this efflorescence, they may be said to blossom with the season. What architectural decoration the buildings carry is not only conventionalized to the point where it is quiet and stays as a sure foil for the nature forms from which it is derived and with which it must intimately associate, but it is always of the surface, never on it.

The windows usually are provided with characteristic straight line patterns absolutely in the flat and usually severe. The nature of the glass is taken into account in these designs as is also the metal bar used in their construction, and most of them are treated as metal „grilles" with glass inserted forming a simple rhytmic arrangement of straight lines and squares as cunning as possible so long as the result is quiet. The aim is that the designs shall make the best of the technical contrivances that produce them.

In the main the ornamentation is wrought in the warp and woof of the structure. It is constitutional in the best sense and is felt in the conception of the ground plan. To elucidate this element in composition would mean a long story and perhaps a tedious one though to me it is the most fascinating phase of the work, involving the true poetry of conception.

The differentiation of a single, certain simple form characterizes the expression of one building. Quite a different form may serve for another, but from one basic idea all the formal elements of design are in each case derived and held well together in scale and character. The form chosen may flare outward, opening flower-like to the sky as in the Thomas house; another droop to accentuate artistically the weight of the masses; another be non-committal or abruptly emphatic, or its grammar may be deduced from some plant form that has appealed to me, as certain properties in line and

form of the sumach were used in the Lawrence house at Springfield; but in every case the motif is adhered to throughout and it is not too much to say that each building æsthetically is „cut from one piece of goods" and consistently hangs together with an integrity impossible otherwise.

In a fine art sense these designs have grown as natural plants grow, the individuality of each is integral and as complete as skill, time, strenght and circumstances permitted.

The method in itself does not of necessity produce a beautiful building, but it provides a framework as a basis which has organic integrity, susceptible to the architect's imagination and at once opening to him Nature's wealth of artistic suggestion, ensuring him a guiding principal within which he can never be wholly false, or lacking in rational motif. The subtleties, the shifting, blending harmonies, cadences, nuances are a matter of his own nature, his own susceptibilities and faculties.

But self denial is imposed upon the architect to a greater extent than upon any member of the fine art family. The temptation to sweeten work, to make each detail in itself lovable and expressive is great; but that the whole may be truly eloquent of its ultimate func-

tion restraint is imperative. To let individual elements shine at the expense of final repose is a betrayal of trust, for buildings are the background or framework for the human life within their walls and a foil for the nature efflorescence without. Architecture is the most complete of conventionalizations and, except music, of all the arts the most subjective.

Music may for the architect be a sympathetic friend whose counsels, precepts and patterns even are available to him and from which he need not fear to draw. But the arts are to-day cursed by literature; artists attempt to make literature of painting and sculpture, even of music, and doubtless would of architecture also, were the art not moribund. Whenever it is done the soul of the thing dies and we have not art but something less for which the artist can have neither affection nor respect. . . .

Contrary to the usual supposition this manner of working out a theme is more flexible than any working out in fixed, historic style can be, and the individuality of those concerned may receive more adequate treatment within legitimate limitations. This matter of „individuality" puzzles many; they suspect that the individuality of the owner and occupant of a building is sacrificed to that of the architect who imposes his own

upon Jones, Brown and Smith alike. An architect worthy of the name has an individuality, it is true; his work will and should reflect it, and his buildings will all bear a family resemblance one to another. The individuality of an owner is first manifest in his choice of his architect, the individual to whom he entrusts his characterization. He sympathizes with his work; its expression suits him and this furnishes the common ground upon which client and architect may come together. Then, if the architect is what he ought to be, with his ready technique he conscientiously works for the client, idealizes his client's character and his client's tastes and makes him feel that the building is his as it really is to such an extent that he can truly say that he would rather have his own house than any he has seen. Is a portrait, say by Sargent, any less a revelation of the character of the subject because it bears his stamp and is easily recognized as a Sargent? Does one lose individuality when interpreted sympathetically by one of his own race and time who can know him and his needs intimately and idealize them; or does one gain it by having adopted to his condition a ready-made historic style which is the fruit of a seedtime other than his, whatever that style may be?

The present industrial condition is constantly studied in the practical application of these architectural ideals and the treatment simplified and arranged to fit modern processes and to utilize to the best advantage the work of the machine. The furniture takes the clean cut, straight-line forms that the machine can render far better than would be possible by hand. Certain facilities, too, of the machine, which it would be interesting to enlarge upon, are taken advantage of and the nature of the materials is usually revealed in the process.

Nor is the atmosphere of the result in its completeness new and hard. In most of the interiors there will be found a quiet, a simple dignity that we imagine is only to be found in the „old" and it is due to the underlying organic harmony, to the each in all and the all in each throughout. This is the modern opportuniy — to make of a building, together with its equipment, appurtenances and environment, an entity which shall constitute a complete work of art, and a work of art more valuable to society as a whole than has before existed because discordant conditions endured for centuries are smoothed away; every-day life here finds an expression germane to its daily existence; an idealization of the common need sure to be uplifting and helpful in the same sense that pure air to breathe is better than air poisoned with noxious gases...

An artist's limitations are his best friends. The machine is here to stay. It is the forerunner of the real democracy that is our dearest hope. There is no more important work before the architect now than to use this normal tool of civilization to the best advantage instead of prostituting it as he has hitherto done in reproducing with murderous ubiquity forms born of other times and other conditions and which it can only serve to destroy.
☐   ☐
The exteriors of these structures will receive less ready recognition perhaps than the interiors and because they are the result of a radically different conception as to what should constitute a building. We have formed a habit of mind concerning architecture to which the expression of most of these exteriors is a shock, at first disagreeable, and the more so as the habit of mind is more narrowly fixed by so called classic training. Our aesthetics are dyspeptic from incontinent indulgence in „Frenchite" pastry. We crave ornament for the sake of ornament; cover up our faults of design with ornamental sensualities that were a long time ago sensuous ornament. I distrust this unwholesome and unholy craving and look to the simple line; to the clean though living form and quiet color for a time, until the true significance of these things has dawned for us once more. The old structural forms which up to the present time, have spelled „architecture" are decayed. Their life went from them long ago and new conditions industrially, steel and concrete and terra cotta in particular, are prophesying a more plastic art wherein as the flesh is to our bones so will the covering be to the structure, but more truly and beautifully expressive than ever. But that too is a long story. Reticence in the matter of ornamentation is characteristic of these structures and for at least two obvious reasons; first, they are the expression of an idea that ornamentation should be constitutional, a matter of the nature of the structure beginning with the ground plan. In the buildings themselves, in the sense of the whole, there is lacking neither richness nor incident but these qualities are secured not by applied decoration, they are found in the fashioning of the whole, in which color, too, plays as significant a part as it does in an old Japanese wood block print. Second; because, as before stated, buildings perform their highest function in relation to human life within and the natural efflorescence without; and to develop and maintain the harmony of a true chord between them making of the building in this sense a sure foil for life, broad, simple surfaces and highly conventionalized forms are inevitable. These ideals take the buildings out of school and marry them to the ground; make them intimate expressions or revelations of the interiors; individualize them regardless of preconceived notions of style. I have tried to make their grammar perfect in its way and to give the forms and proportions an integrity that will bear study, although few of them can be intelligently studied apart from their environment. So, what might be termed the democratic character of the exteriors is their first undefined offence— the lack, wholly, of what the professional critic would deem architecture; in fact, most of the critic's architecture has been left out.
There is a synthetic basis for the features of the various structures, and consequently a constantly accumulating residue of formulae, which becomes more and more useful; but I do not pretend to say that perception or

conception was not at first intuitive, or that what lies yet beyond will not be grasped in the same intuitive way; but, after all, architecture is a scientific art, and the thinking basis will ever be for the architect his surety, the final court in which his imagination sifts his feelings...

The few draughtsmen so far associated with this work have been taken into the draughting room, in every case almost wholly unformed, many of them with no particular previous training, and patiently nursed for years in the atmosphere of the work itself, until, saturated by intimate association, at an impressionable age, with its motifs and phases, they have become helpful. To develop the sympathetic grasp of detail that is necessary before this point is reached has proved usually a matter of years, with little advantage on the side of the college-trained understudy. These young people have found their way to me through natural sympathy with the work, and have become loyal assistants. The members, so far, all told here and elsewhere, of our little university of fourteen year's standing are: Marion Mahony, a capable assistant for eleven years; William Drummond, for seven years; Francis Byrne, five years; Isabel Roberts, five years; George Willis, four years; Walter Griffin, four years; Andrew Willatzen, three years; Harry Robinson, two years; Charles E. White, Jr., one year; Erwin Barglebaugh and Robert Hardin, each one year; Albert McArthur, entering.

Others have been attracted by what seemed to them to be the novelty of the work, staying only long enough to acquire a smattering of form, then departing to sell a superficial proficiency elsewhere. Still others shortly develop a mastery of the subject, discovering that it

is all just as they would have done it, anyway, and, chafing at the unkind fate that forestalled them in its practice, resolve to blaze a trail for themselves without further loss of time. It is urged against the more loyal that they are sacrificing their individuality to that which has dominated this work; but it is too soon to impeach a single understudy on this basis, for, although they will inevitably repeat for years the methods, forms and habit of thought, even the mannerisms of the present work, if there is virtue in the principles behind it that virtue will stay with them through the preliminary stages of their own practice until their own individualities truly develop independently. I have noticed that those who have made the most fuss about their „individuality" in early stages, those who took themselves most seriously in that regard, were inevitably those who had least. Many elements of Mr. Sullivan's personality in his art— what might be called his mannerisms—naturally enough clung to my work in the early years, and may be readily traced by the casual observer; but for me one real proof of the virtue inherent in this work will lie in the fact that some of the young men and women who have given themselves up to me so faithfully these past years will some day contribute rounded individualities of their own, and forms of their own devising to the new school. This year I assign to each a project that has been carefully conceived in my own mind, which he accepts as a specific work. He follows its subsequent development through all its phases in drawing room and field, meeting with the client himself on occasion, gaining an allround development impossible otherwise, and insuring an enthusiasm and a grasp of detail decidedly to the best interest of the client. These privileges in

the hands of selfishly ambitious or over-confident assistants would soon wreck such a system; but I can say that among my own boys it has so far proved a moderate success, with prospect of being continued as a settled policy in future.

Nevertheless, I believe that only when one individual forms the concept of the various projects and also determines the character of every detail in the sum total, even to the size and shape of the pieces of glass in the windows, the arrangement and profile of the most insignificant of the architectural members, will that unity be secured which is the soul of the individual work of art. This means that fewer buildings should be entrusted to one architect. His output will of necessity be relatively small-small, that is, as compared to the volume of work turned out in any one of fifty „successful" offices in America. I believe there is no middle course worth considering in the light of the best future of American architecture. With no more propriety can an architect leave the details touching the handling of his conception to assistants, no matter how sympathetic and capable they may be, than can a painter entrust the painting in of the details of his picture to a pupil; for an architect who would do individual work must have a technique well developed and peculiar to himself, which, if he is fertile, is still growing with his growth. To keep everyting „in place" requires constant care and study in matters that the old-school practitioner would scorn to touch. . . .

As for the future-the work shall grow more truly simple; more expressive with fewer lines, fewer forms; more articulate with less labor; more plastic; more fluent, although more coherent; more organic. It shall grow not only to fit more perfectly the methods and processes that are called upon to produce it, but shall further find whatever is lovely or of good repute in method or process, and idealize it with the cleanest, most virile stroke I can imagine. As understanding and appreciation of life matures and deepens, this work shall prophesy and idealize the character of the individual it is fashioned to serve more intimately, no matter how inexpensive the result must finally be. It shall become in its atmosphere as pure and elevating in its humble way as the trees and flowers are in their perfectly appointed way, for only so can architecture be worthy its high rank as a fine art, or the architect discharge the obligation he assumes to the public-imposed upon him by the nature of his own profession.

IN THE CAUSE OF ARCHITECTURE
☐ ☐ BY FRANK LLOYD WRIGHT ☐ ☐

SECOND PAPER   MAY 1914

"Nature has made creatures only; Art has made men."
Nevertheless, or perhaps for that very reason, every
struggle for truth in the arts and for the freedom that
should go with the truth has always had its own peculiar load of disciples, neophytes and quacks. The young
work in architecture here in the Middle West, owing to
a measure of premature success, has for some time
past been daily rediscovered, heralded and drowned in
noise by this now characteristic feature of its struggle.
The so-called "movement" threatens to explode soon
in foolish exploitation of unripe performances or topple
over in pretentious attempts to "speak the language."
The broker, too, has made his appearance to deal in
its slender stock in trade, not a wholly new form of
artistic activity certainly, but one serving to indicate
how profitable this intensive rush for a place in the
"new school" has become.
Just at this time it may be well to remember that "every
form of artistic activity is not Art."
Obviously this stage of development was to be expected
and has its humorous side. It has also unexpected and
dangerous effects, astonishingly in line with certain
prophetic letters written by honest "conservatives" upon
the publication of the former paper of 1908.
Although an utterance from me of a critical nature is
painful, because it must be a personal matter, perhaps
a seeming retraction on my part, still all that ever really

happens is "personal matter" and the time has come
when forbearance ceases to be either virtue or con-
venience. A promising garden seems to be rapidly
overgrown with weeds notwithstanding the fact that
"all may raise the flowers now, for all have got the
seed." But the seed has not been planted — transplanting
is preferred, but it cannot raise the needed flowers.
To stultify or corrupt our architectural possibilities is
to corrupt our æsthetic life at the fountain head.
Her Architecture is the most precious of the susceptibilities of a young, constructive country in this constructive
stage of development and maintaining its integrity in
this respect therefore, distinctly a cause.
When, twenty-one years ago, I took my stand, alone in
my field, the cause was unprofitable, seemingly impossible, almost unknown, or, if known, was, as a rule, unho-
nored and ridiculed — Montgomery Schuyler was the one
notable exception to the rule. So swiftly do things "come
on" in this vigorous and invigorating age that although
the cause itself has had little or no recognition, the
work has more than its share of attention and has
attracted to itself abuses seldom described — never openly
attacked — but which a perspective of the past six years
will enable me to describe, as I feel they must render
the finer values in this work abortive for the time being,
if they do not wholly defeat its aim. Many a similar
work in the past has gone prematurely to ruin owing
to similar abuses — to rise again, it is true, but retarded
generations in time.
I still believe that the ideal of an organic *) architecture

*) By organic architecture I mean an architecture that develops from within outward
in harmony with the conditions of its being as distinguished from one that is applied
from without.

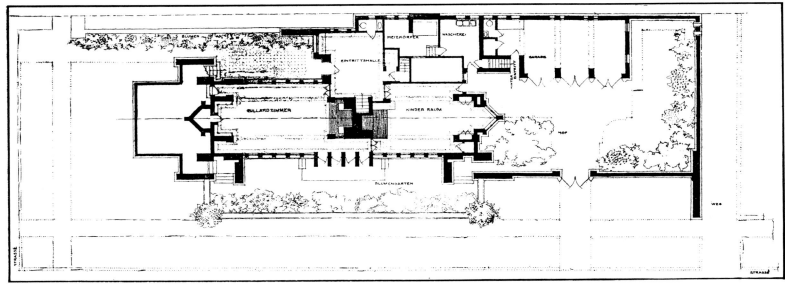

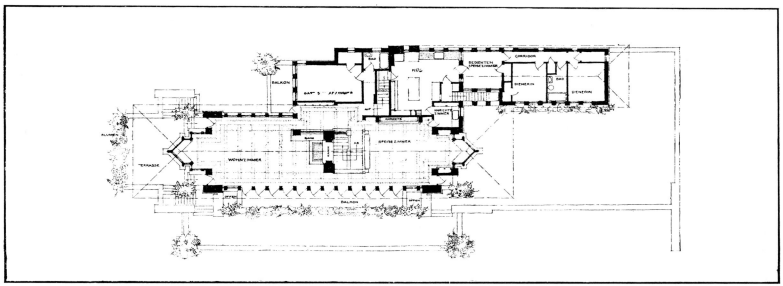

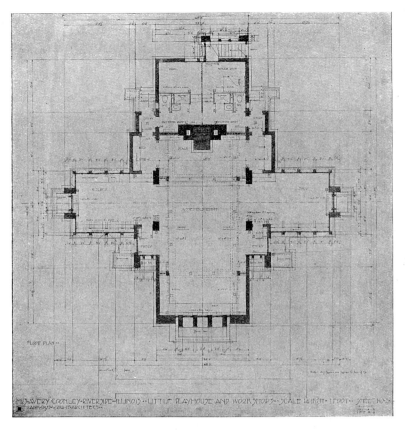

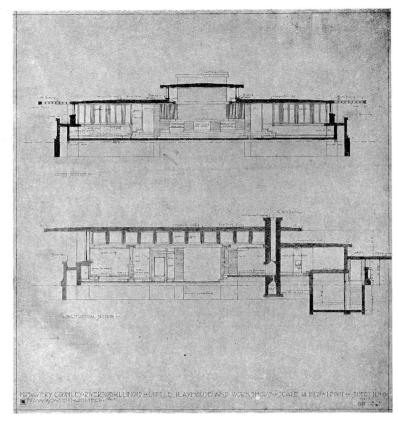

forms the origin and source, the strength and, fundamentally, the significance of everything ever worthy the name of architecture.

And I know that the sense of an organic architecture, once grasped, carries with it in its very nature the discipline of an ideal and at whatever cost to self interest or the established order.

It is itself a standard and an ideal.

And I maintain that only earnest artist integrity, both of instinct and of intelligence, can make any forward movement of this nature in architecture of lasting value. The ideal of an organic architecture for America is no mere license for doing the thing that you please to do as you please to do it in order to hold up the strange thing when done with the "see-what-I-have-made" of childish pride. Nor is it achieved by speaking the fancied language of "form and function" — cant terms learned by rote — or prating foolishly of "Progress before Precedent" — that unthinking, unthinkable thing! In fact, it is precisely the total absence of any conception of this ideal standard that is made conspicuous by this folly and the practices that go with it.

To reiterate the statement made in 1908: This ideal of an organic architecture for America was touched by Richardson and Root, and perhaps other men, but was developing consciously twenty-eight years ago in the practice of Adler & Sullivan, when I went to work in their office. This ideal combination of Adler & Sullivan was then working to produce what no other combination of architects nor any individual architect at that time dared even preach — a sentient, rational building that would owe its "style" to the integrity with which it was individually fashioned to serve its particular purpose — a "thinking" as well as "feeling" process, requiring the independent work of true artist imagination —

an ideal that is dynamite, cap and fuse, in selfish, insensible hands — personal ambition, the lighted match. At the expiration of a six year apprenticeship, during which time Louis Sullivan was my master and inspiration, twenty-one years ago, I entered a field he had not, in any new spirit, touched — the field of domestic architecture — and began to break ground and make the forms I needed, alone — absolutely alone. These forms were the result of a conscientious study of materials and of the machine which is the real tool, whether we like it or not, that we must use to give shape to our ideals — a tool which at that time had received no such artistic consideration from artist or architect. And that my work now has individuality, the strength to stand by itself, honors Mr. Sullivan the more. The principles, however, underlying the fundamental ideal of an organic architecture, common to his work and to mine, are common to all work that ever rang true in the architecture of the world, and free as air to any pair of honest young lungs that will breathe deeply enough. But I have occasion to refer here only to that element in this so-called "new movement" which I have characterized by my own work and which should and, in a more advanced stage of culture, would be responsible to me for use or abuse of the forms and privileges of that work. Specifically, I speak only to that element within this element, now beyond private reach or control, ruthlessly characterizing and publicly exploiting the cause it does not comprehend or else that it cannot serve. Some one for the sake of that cause must have some conscience in the matter and tell the truth. Since disciples, neophytes and brokers will not, critics do not, and the public cannot — I will. I will be suspected of the unbecoming motives usually ascribed to any man who comes to the front in behalf of an ideal or his own;

nevertheless, somehow, this incipient movement, which it has been my life work to help outfit and launch, must be protected or directed in its course. An enlightened public opinion would take care of this, but there is no such opinion. In time there will be; meantime good work is being wasted, opportunities destroyed or worse, architectural mortgages on future generations forged wholesale; and in architecture they must be paid with usurious interest.

The sins of the Architect are permanent sins.

To promote good work it is necessary to characterize bad work as bad.

Half-baked, imitative designs — fictitious semblances — pretentiously put forward in the name of a movement or a cause, particularly while novelty is the chief popular standard, endanger the cause, weaken the efficacy of genuine work, for the time being at least, lower the standard of artistic integrity permanently, demoralize all values artistically, until utter prostitution results. This prostitution has resulted in the new work partly, I have now to confess, as a by-product of an intimate, personal touch with the work, hitherto untried in the office of an American architect; and partly, too, perhaps, as one result of an ideal of individuality in architecture, administered in doses too strong, too soon, for architectural babes and sucklings; but chiefly, I believe, owing to almost total lack of any standard of artist integrity among architects, as a class, in this region at least. Of ethics we hear something occasionally, but only in regard to the relation of architects to each other when a client is in question—never in relation to sources of inspiration, the finer material the architect uses in shaping the thing he gives to his client. Ethics that

promote integrity in this respect are as yet unformed and the young man in architecture is adrift in the most vitally important of his experiences, he cannot know where he stands in the absence of any well-defined principles on the part of his conferers or his elders. If I had a right to project myself in the direction of an organic architecture twenty-one years ago, then it entailed the right to my work and so far as I am able, a right to defend my aim. Also—yet not so clearly— I am bound to do what I can to save the public from untoward effects that follow in the wake of my own break with traditions. I deliberately chose to break with traditions in order to be more true to Tradition than current conventions and ideals in architecture would permit. The more vital course is usually the rougher one and lies through conventions oftentimes settled into laws that must be broken, with consequent liberation of other forces that cannot stand freedom. So a break of this nature is a thing dangerous nevertheless indispensable to society. Society recognizes the danger and makes the break usually fatal to the man who makes it. It should not be made without reckoning the danger and sacrifice, without ability to stand severe punishment, nor without sincere faith that the end will justify the means; nor do I believe it can be effectively made without all these. But who can reckon with the folly bred by temporal success in a country that has as yet no artistic standards, no other god so potent as that same Success? For every thousand men nature enables to stand adversity, she, perhaps, makes one man capable of surviving success. An unenlightened public is at its mercy always—the „success" of the one thousand as well as of the one in a thousand; were it not for the resistance

□ □ LITTLE □ □
PLAYHOUSE
MRS: COONLEY
□ 1LLINOIS □

of honest enmity, society, nature herself even, would soon cycle madly to disaster. So reaction is essential to progress, and enemies as valuable an asset in any forward movement as friends, provided only they be honest; if intelligent as well as honest, they are invaluable. Some time ago this work reached the stage where it sorely needed honest enemies if it was to survive. It has had some honest enemies whose honest fears were expressed in the prophetic letters I have mentioned.

But the enemies of this work, with an exception or two, have not served it well. They have been either unintelligent or careless of the gist of the whole matter. In fact, its avowed enemies have generally been of the same superficial, time serving spirit as many of its present load of disciples and neophytes. Nowhere even now, save in Europe, with some few notable exceptions in this country, has the organic character of the work been fairly recognized and valued—the character that is perhaps the only feature of lasting vital consequence. As for its peculiarities—if my own share in this work has a distinguished trait, it has individuality undefiled. It has gone forward unswerving from the beginning, unchanging, yet developing, in this quality of individuality,

and stands, as it has stood for nineteen years at least, an individual entity, clearly defined. Such as it is, its "individuality" is as irrevocably mine as the work of any painter, sculptor or poet who ever lived was irrevocably his. The form of a work that has this quality of individuality is never the product of a composite. An artist knows this; but the general public, near artist, and perhaps "critic", too, may have to be reminded or informed. To grant a work this quality is to absolve it without further argument from anything like composite origin, and to fix its limitations.

There are enough types and forms in my work to characterize the work of an architect, but certainly not enough to characterize an architecture. Nothing to my mind could be worse imposition than to have some individual, even temporarily, deliberately fix the outward forms of his concept of beauty upon the future of a free people or even of a growing city. A tentative, advantageous forecast of probable future utilitarian development goes far enough in this direction. Any individual willing to undertake more would thereby only prove his unfitness for the task, assuming the task possible or desirable. A socialist might shut out the sunlight from a free and developing people with his own shadow, in

this way. An artist is too true an individualist to suffer such an imposition, much less perpetrate it: his problems are quite other. The manner of any work (and all work of any quality has its manner) may be for the time being a strength, but finally it is a weakness; and as the returns come in, it seems as though not only the manner of this work or its "clothes," but also its strength in this very quality of individuality, which is a matter of its soul as well as of its forms, would soon prove its undoing, to be worn to shreds and tatters by foolish, conscienceless imitation. As for the vital principle of the work—the quality of an organic architecture—that has been lost to sight, even by pupils. But I still believe as firmly as ever that without artist integrity and this consequent individuality manifesting itself in multifarious forms, there can be no great architecture, no great artists, no great civilization, no worthy life. Is, then, the very strength of such a work as this is its weakness? Is it so because of a false democratic system naturally inimical to art? or is it so because the commercialization of art leaves no noble standards? Is it because architects have less personal honor than sculptors, painters, or poets? Or is it because fine buildings are less important now than fine pictures and good books?

In any case, judging from what is exploited as such, most of what is beginning to be called the "New School of the Middle West", is not only far from the ideal of an organic architecture, but getting farther away from it every day.

A study of similar situations in the past will show that any departure from beaten paths must stand and grow in organic character or soon fall, leaving permanent waste and desolation in final ruin: it dare not trade long on mere forms, no matter how inevitable they seem. Trading in the letter has cursed art for centuries past, but in architecture it has usually been rather an impersonal letter, of those decently cold in their graves for some time.

One may submit to the flattery of imitation or to caricature personally; every one who marches or strays from beaten paths must submit to one or to both, but never will he submit tamely to caricature of that which he loves. Personally, I, too, am heartily sick of being commercialized and traded in and upon; but most of all I dread to see the types I have worked with so long and patiently drifting toward speculative builders, cheapened or befooled by senseless changes, robbed of quality and distinction, dead forms or grinning origina-

lities for the sake of originality, an endless string of hacked carcasses, to encumber democratic front yards for five decades or more. I now often turn with a feeling of disgust from my work; but I can give it up no more than I can stop breathing — I can only do both at the same time.

It would require a superhuman effort on my part to lay these types aside, let them go to the destitute and prostitute, and undertake to invest new ones necessary to prolong the life of a "Movement" for any length of time. Grammar and all—they represent my own feeling, thought and experience. It would be like sloughing my skin and at the age of forty-six starting to grow a new one. And why should I? This. however, is only the personal side of the matter and to be endured in silence were there any profit in it to come to the future architecture of the "melting pot."

The more serious side and the occasion for this second paper is the fact that emboldened or befooled by its measure of "Success", the new work has been showing weaknesses instead of the character it might have shown some years hence were it more enlightened and discreet, more sincere and modest, prepared to wait, to wait to prepare.

The average American man or woman who wants to build a house wants something different—"something different" is what they say they want and most of them want it in a hurry. That this is the fertile soil upon which an undisciplined "language speaking" neophyte may grow his crop to the top of his ambition is deplorable in one sense, but none the less hopeful in another and more vital sense. The average man of business in America has truer intuition and so a more nearly just estimate of artistic values, when he has a chance to judge between good and bad, than a man of similar class in any other country. But he is prone to take that "something different" anyhow; if not good, then bad. He is rapidly outgrowing the provincialism that needs a foreign-made label upon "Art", and so, at the present moment, not only is he in danger of being swindled,

but likely to find something peculiarly his own, in time, and valuable to him, if he can last. I hope and believe he can last. At any rate, there is no way of preventing him from getting either swindled or something merely "different"; nor do I believe it would be desirable if he could be, until the inorganic thing he usually gets in the form of this "something different" is put forward and publicly advertised as of that character of the young work for which I must feel myself responsible.

I do not admit that my disciples or pupils, be they artists, neophytes, or brokers, are responsible for worse buildings than nine-tenths of the work done by average architects who are "good school"—in fact, I think the worst of them do better—although they sometimes justify themselves in equivocal positions by reference to this fact. Were no more to come of my work than is evident at present, the architecture of the country would have received an impetus that will finally resolve itself into good. But to me the exasperating fact is that it might aid vitally the great thing we all desire, if it were treated

on its merits, used, and not abused. Selling even good versions of an original, at second-hand, is in the circumstances not good enough. It is cheap and bad— demoralizing in every sense. But, unhappily, I have to confess that the situation seems worse where originality, as such, has thus far been attempted, because it seems to have been attempted chiefly for its own sake, and the results bear about the same resemblance to an organic architecture as might be shown were one to take a classic column and, breaking it, let the upper half lie carelessly at the foot of the lower, then setting the capital picturesquely askew against the half thus prostrate, one were to settle the whole arrangement as some structural feature of street or garden.

For worker or broker to exhibit such "designs" as efforts of creative architects, before the ink is yet dry on either work or worker, is easily done under present standards with "success," but the exploit finally reflects a poor sort of credit upon the exploited architect and the cause. As for the cause, any growth that comes to

it in a "spread" of this kind is unwholesome. I insist that this sort of thing is not "new school", nor this the way to develop one. This is piracy, lunacy, plunder, imitation, adulation, or what you will; it is not a developing architecture when worked in this fashion, nor will it ever become one until purged of this spirit; least of all is it an organic architecture. Its practices belie any such character.

"Disciples" aside, some fifteen young people, all entirely inexperienced and unformed—but few had even college educations—attracted by the character of my work, sought me as their employer. I am no teacher; I am a worker—but I gave to all, impartially, the freedom of my work room, my work and myself, to imbue them with the spirit of the performances for their own sakes, and with the letter for my sake, so that they might become useful to me, because the nature of my endeavor was such that I had to train my own help and pay current wages while I trained them. In a former paper, bearing the same caption as this one, I referred to the work as a small university and latterly in that spirit it was carried on for a time. It seemed to me that I could best serve the future of a developing architecture by developing my assistants in that spirit.

The nature of the profession these young people were to make when they assumed to practice architecture, entails much more careful preparation than that of the "good school" architect; theirs is a far more difficult thing to do technically and artistically, if they would do something of their own. To my chagrin, too many are content to take it "ready made" and with no further preparation hasten to compete for clients of their own. Now fifteen good, bad and indifferent are practicing architecture in the Middle West, South and far West, and with considerable "success". In common with the work of numerous disciples, (judging from such work as has been put forward publicly), there is a restless jockeying with members, one left off here, another added there, with varying intent—in some, a vain endeavor to re-individualize the old types; in others, an attempt to conceal their origin, but always—ad nauseam—the inevitable reiteration of the features that gave the original work its style and individuality. To find fault with this were unfair. It is not unexpected nor unpromising except in those unbearable cases where badly modified inorganic results seem to satisfy their authors' conception of originality; and banalities of form and proportion are accordingly advertised in haste as work of creative architects of a "new school." That some uniformity in performance should have obtained for some years is natural; it could not be otherwise, unless unaware I had harbored marked genuises. But when the genius arrives, nobody will take his work for mine—least of all will he mistake my work for his.

"The letter killeth." In this young work at this time, still it is the letter that killeth, and emulation of the "letter" that gives the illusion or delusion of "movement". There is no doubt, however, but that the sentiment is awakened which will mean progressive movement in time. And there are many working quietly, who, I am sure, will give a good account of themselves.

Meanwhile, the spirit in which this use of the letter has its rise is important to any noble future still left to the cause. If the practices that disgrace and demoralize the soul of the young man in architecture could be made plain to him; if he could be shown that inevitably equi-

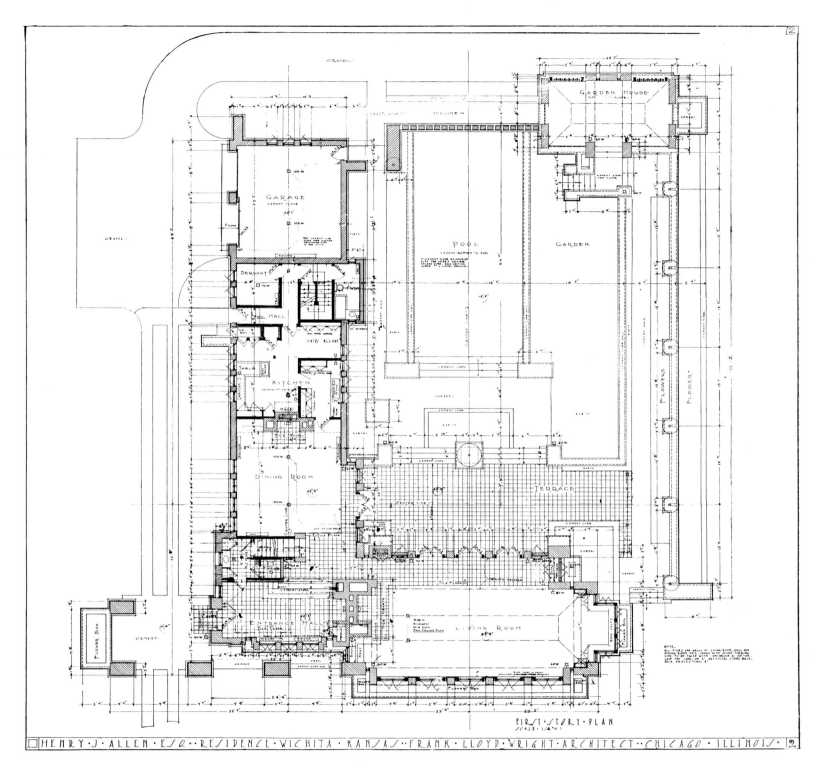

FIRST·STORY·PLAN
SCALE: 1/4" = 1'

HENRY·J·ALLEN·ESQ·RESIDENCE·WICHITA·KANSAS·FRANK·LLOYD·WRIGHT·ARCHITECT·CHICAGO·ILLINOIS

vocation dwarfs and eventually destroys what creative faculty he may possess—that designing lies in design to deceive one's self or others,—one by one shut him out absolutely from realizing upon his own gifts—no matter how flattering his opportunities may be—if he could realize that the artist heart is one uncompromising core of truth in seeking, in giving, or in taking—a precious service could be rendered him. The young architect who is artist enough to know where he stands and man enough to use honestly his parent forms as

such, conservatively, until he feels his own strength within him, is only exercising an artistic birthright in the interest of a good cause—he has the character at least from which great things may come. But the boy who steals his forms—"steals" them because he sells them as his own for the moment of superficial distinction he gains by trading on the results—is no artist, has not the sense of the first principles of the ideal that he poses and the forms that he abuses. He denies his birthright, an act characteristic and unimportant; but for a mess

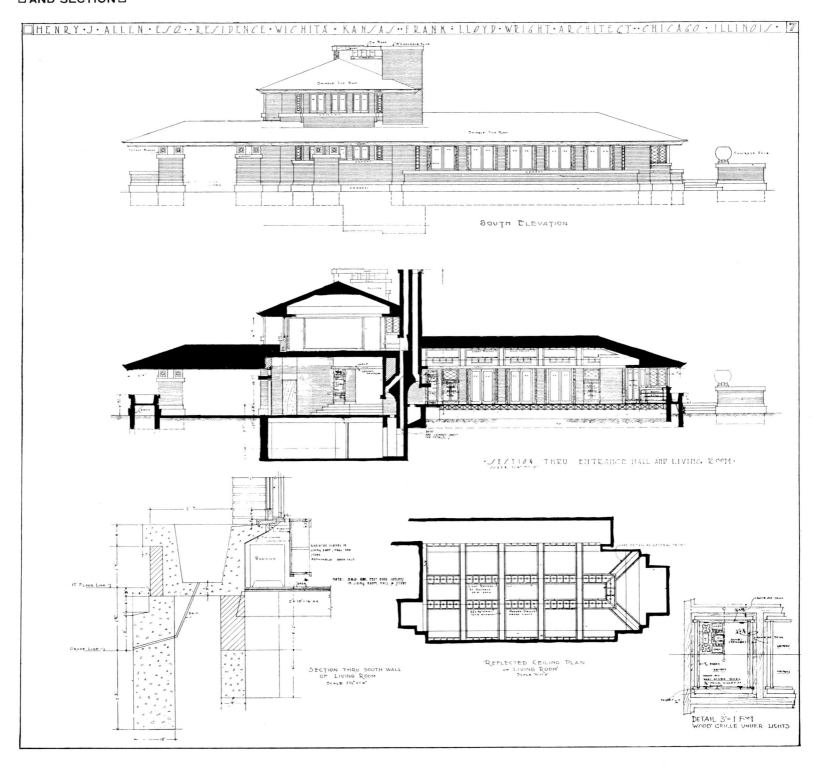

·HENRY·J·ALLEN·ESQ·RESIDENCE·WICHITA·KANSAS·FRANK·LLOYD·WRIGHT·ARCHITECT·CHICAGO·ILLINOIS·

SOUTH ELEVATION

·SECTION THRU ENTRANCE HALL AND LIVING ROOM·

SECTION THRU SOUTH WALL
OF LIVING ROOM
SCALE 1½"=1'0"

·REFLECTED CEILING PLAN
OF LIVING ROOM·
SCALE ¾"=1'0"

DETAIL 3"=1 FOOT
WOOD GRILLE UNDER LIGHTS

of pottage, he endangers the chances of a genuine forward movement, insults both cause and precedent with an astounding insolence quite peculiar to these matters in the United States, ruthlessly sucks what blood may be left in the tortured and abused forms he caricatures and exploits—like the parasite he is.

A condition as far removed from creative work is the state of mind of those who, having in the course of their day's labor put some stitches into the "clothes" of the work, assume, therefore, that style and pattern are rightfully theirs and wear them defiantly unregenerate. The gist of the whole matter artistically has entirely eluded them. This may be the so-called "democratic" point of view; at any rate, it is the immemorial error of the rabble. No great artist nor work of art ever proceeded from that conception, nor ever will.

Then there is the soiled and soiling fringe of all creative effort, a type common to all work everywhere that meets with any degree of success, although it may be more virulent here because of low standards; those who

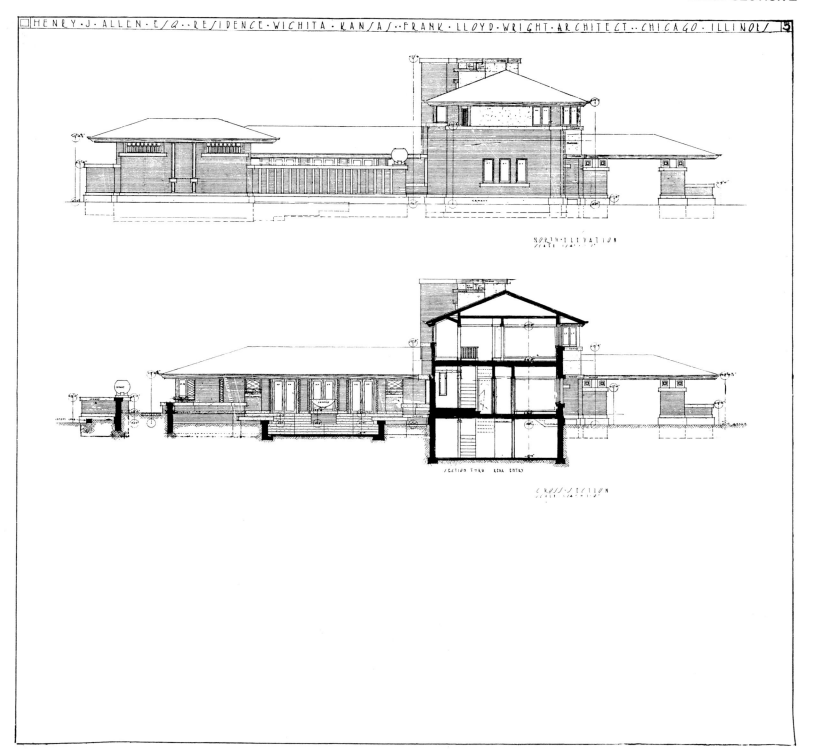

□ HENRY·J·ALLEN·E/Q··RE/IDENCE·WICHITA·KAN/A/··FRANK·LLOYD·WRIGHT·ARCHITECT··CHICAGO··ILLINOI/ □ 5

NORTH·ELEVATION

/ECTION THRU REAR ENTRY

CROSS·SECTION

benefit by the use of another's work and to justify themselves depreciate both the work and worker they took it from—the type that will declare, „In the first place, I never had your shovel; in the second place, I never broke your shovel; and in the third place, it was broken when I got it, anyway"—the type that with more crafty intelligence develops into the "coffin worm." One of Whistler's „coffin worms" has just wriggled in and out. But underneath all, I am constrained to believe, lies the feverish ambition to get fame or fortune "quick," cha-racteristic of the rush of commercial standards that rule in place of artist standards and consequent unwilling-ness to wait to prepare thoroughly.

"Art to one is high as a heavenly goddess; to another only the thrifty cow that gives him his butter," said Schiller; and who will deny that our profession is pros-titute to the cow, meager in ideals, cheap in perfor-mance, commercial in spirit; demoralized by ignoble ambition! A foolish optimism regarding this only serves to perpetuate it. Foolish optimism and the vanity of fear

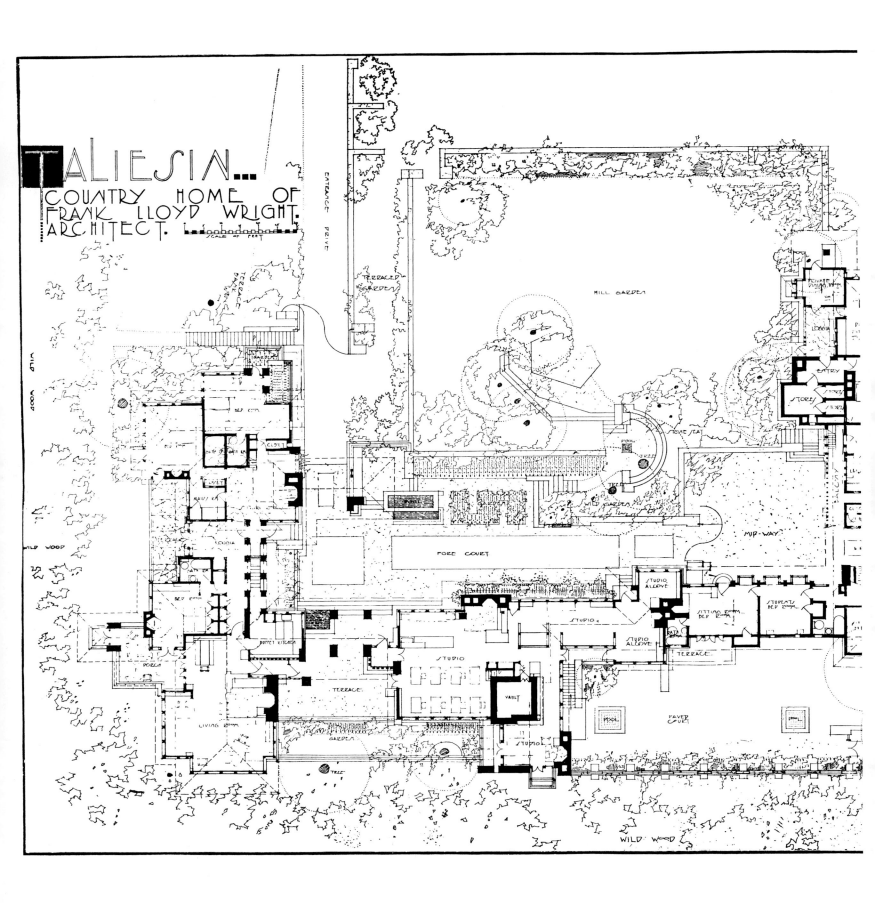

TALIESIN...
COUNTRY HOME OF
FRANK LLOYD WRIGHT.
ARCHITECT.

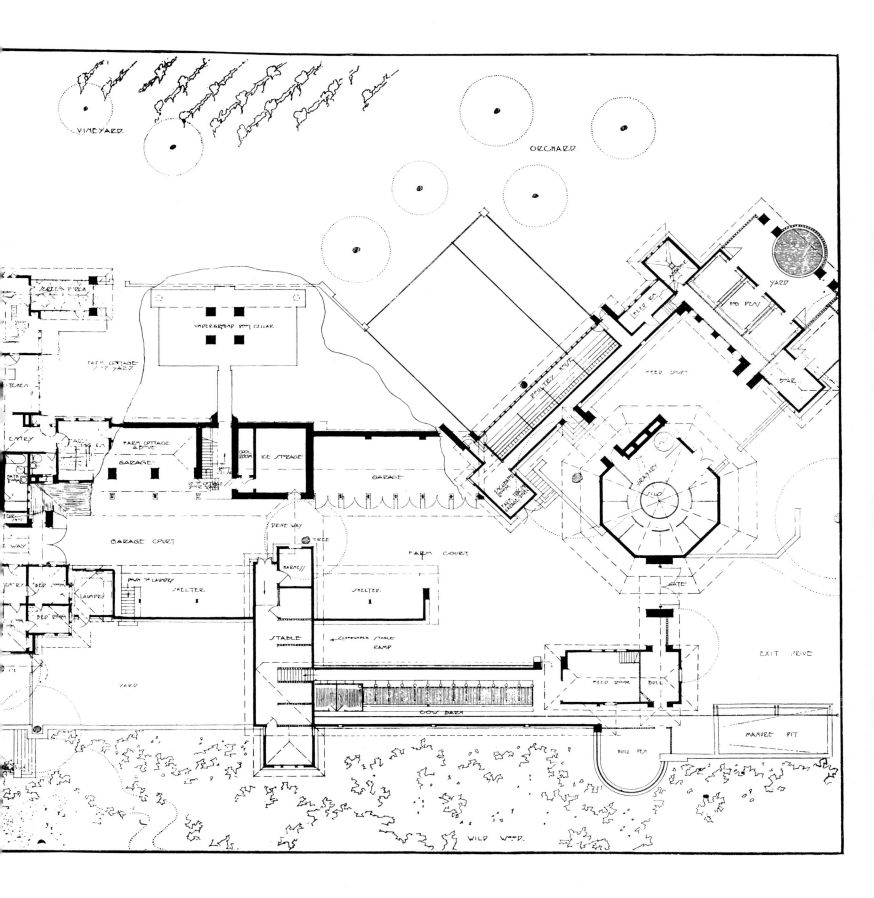

VINEYARD.

ORCHARD

YARD

UNDERGROUND ROOT CELLAR.

FARM COTTAGE 2ND YARD

KITCHEN

ENTRY

FARM COTTAGE ABOVE

GARAGE

COOL ROOM

ICE STORAGE

GARAGE

FEED COURT

POULTRY RUN

FEED RM

HEN PLAN

BARN

SILO

GRANARY

GARAGE COURT

DRIVE WAY

TREE

FARM COURT

GATE

WAY

BARNS

SHELTER

SHELTER

DOWN TO LAUNDRY

BED ROOM

LAUNDRY

EXIT DRIVE

STABLE

COWS WATER STABLE

RAMP

FEED ROOM

BULL

YARD

COW BARN

MANURE PIT

BULL PEN

WILD WOOD.

of ridicule or "failure" are both friends of ignorance. In no country in the world do disciples, neophytes, or brokers pass artist counterfeit so easily as in these United States. Art is commercialized here rather more than anything else, although the arts should be as free from this taint as religion. But has religion escaped? So the standard of criticism is not only low—it is often dishonest or faked somewhere between the two, largely manufactured to order for profit or bias. Criticism is worked as an advertising game, traders' instincts subject to the prevailing commercial taint. Therein lies a radically evil imposition that harms the public; that also further distorts, confuses, and injures values and promotes bad work; that tends to render the integrity of artist and commerce alike a stale and unprofitable joke, and to make honest enemies even harder to find than honest friends. The spirit of fair play, the endeavor to preserve the integrity of values, intelligently, on a high plane in order to help in raising the level of the standard of achievement in the country, and to refrain from throwing the senseless weight of the mediocre and bad upon it—all this is unhappily too rare among editors. The average editor has a "constituency," not a standard. This constituency is largely the average architect who has bought the "artistic" in his architecture as one of its dubious and minor aspects, or the sophisticated neophyte, the broker and the quack to whom printers' ink is ego-balm and fortune.

So until the standard is raised any plea for artist integrity is like a cry for water in the Painted Desert. As for competent, criticism, the honest word of illuminating insight, where is it? Nothing is more precious or essential to progress. Where is the editor or critic not narrow or provincial? Or loose and ignorant? Or cleverly or superficially, or cowardly commercial? Let him raise his standard! Friend or foe, there is still a demand for

SEATDESK AND BOOKCASE   TALIESIN   SCALE 1½ INCH EQUALS 1 FOOT

ELEVATION

him even here; but if he did, he would fail—gloriously fail—of "success."

Is architecture, then, no longer to be practiced as an art? Has its practice permanently descended to a form of mere "artistic activity"?

The art of architecture has fallen from a high estate—lower steadily since the Men of Florence patched together fragments of the art of Greece and Rome and in vain endeavor to re-establish its eminence manufactured the Renaissance. It has fallen—from the heavenly Goddess of Antiquity and the Middle Ages to the thrifty cow of the present day. To touch upon these matters in this country is doubly unkind, for it is to touch upon the question of "bread and butter" chiefly. Aside from the conscienceless ambition of the near artist—more sordid than any greed of gold—and beneath this thin pretense of the ideal that veneers the curious compound of broker and neophyte, there lurks, I know, for any young architect

an ever present dread of the kind of "failure" that is the obverse of the kind of "success" that commercialized standards demand of him if he is to survive. Whosoever would worship his heavenly goddess has small choice—he must keep his eye on the thrifty cow or give up his dream of "success;" and the power of discrimination possessed by the cow promises ill for the future integrity of an organic architecture. The net result of present standards is likely to be a poor wretch, a coward who aspires pretentiously or theoretically, advertises cleverly and milks surreptitiously. There is no real connection between aspiration and practice except a tissue of lies and deceit; there never can be. The young architect before he ventures to practice architecture with an ideal, to-day, should first be sure of his goddess and then, somehow, be connected with a base of supplies from which he cannot be cut off, or else fall in with the rank and file of the "good school" of the hour. Any

one who has tried it knows this; that is, if he is honest and is going to use his own material as soon as he is able. So the ever present economic question underlies this question of artist integrity, at this stage of our development, like quicksand beneath the footing of a needed foundation, and the structure itself seems doomed to shreds and cracks and shores and patches, the deadening compromises, and pitiful makeshifts of the struggle to succeed! Even the cry for this integrity will bind the legion together, as one man, against the crier and the cry.

This is Art, then, is a sentimental Democracy, which seems to be only another form of self same hypocrisy? Show me a man who prates of such "Democracy" as a basis for artist endeavor, and I will show you an inordinately foolish egotist or a quack. The "Democracy" of the man in the American street is no more than the Gospel of Mediocrity. When it is understood that a great Democracy is the highest form of Aristocracy conceivable, not of birth or place or wealth, but of those qualities that give distinction to the man as a man, and that as a social state it must be characterized by the honesty and responsibility of the absolute individualist as the unit of its structure, then only can we have an Art worthy the name. The rule of mankind by mankind is one thing; but false "Democracy"—the hypocritical sentimentality, politically practiced and preached here, usually the sheep's clothing of the proverbial wolf, or the egotistic dream of self-constitued patron saints—is quite another thing. "The letter killeth;" yes, but more deadly

still is the undertow of false democracy, that poses the man as a creative artist and starves him to death unless he fakes his goddess or persuades himself, with "language," that the cow is really she. Is the lack of an artist-conscience, then, simply the helpless surrender of the would-be artist to this where-withal Democracy with which a notion soothes itself into subjection? Is the integrity for which I plead here no part of this time and place? And is no young aspirant or hardened sinner to blame for lacking it? It may be so. If it is, we can at least be honest about that, too. But what aspiring artist could knowingly face such a condition? He would choose to dig in the ditch and trace his dreams by lamplight, on scrap paper, for the good of his own soul—a sweet and honorable, if commercially futile, occupation. It has been my hope to have inspired among my pupils

a personality or two to contribute to this work, some day, forms of their own devising, with an artistic integrity that will help to establish upon a firmer basis the efforts that have gone before them and enable them in more propitious times to carry on their practice with a personal gentleness, wisdom, and reverence denied to the pioneers who broke rough ground for them, with a wistful eye to better conditions for their future.

And I believe that, cleared of the superficial pose and push that is the inevitable abuse of its opportunity and its nature, and against which I ungraciously urge myself here, there will be found good work in a cause that deserves honest friends and honest enemies among the better architects of the country. Let us have done with "language" and unfair; use of borrowed forms understand that such practices or products are not of

the character of this young work. This work is a sincere endeavor to establish the ideal of an organic architecture in a new country; a type of endeavor that alone can give lasting value to any architecture and that is in line with the spirit of every great and noble precedent in the world of forms that has come to us as the heritage of the great life that has been lived, and in the spirit of which all great life to be will still be lived.

And this thing that eludes the disciple, remains in hiding from the neophyte, and in the name of which the broker seduces his client—what is it? This mystery requiring the catch phrases of a new language to abate the agonies of the convert and in the name of which ubiquitous atrocities have been and will continue to be committed, with the deadly enthusiasm of the ego-mania that is its plague? First, a study of the nature of materials you elect to use and the tools you must use them with, searching to find the characteristic qualities in both that are suited to your purpose. Second, with an ideal of organic nature as a guide, so to unite these qualities to serve that purpose, that the fashion of what you do has integrity or is natively fit, regardless of preconceived notions of style. Style is a by-product of the process and comes of the man or the mind in the process. The style of the thing, therefore, will be the man—it is his. Let his forms alone.

To adopt a "style" as a motive is to put the cart before the horse and get nowhere beyond the "Styles"—never to reach Style.

It is obvious that this is neither ideal nor work for fakers

or tyros; for unless this process is finally so imbued, informed, with a feeling for the beautiful that grace and proportion are inevitable, the result cannot get beyond good engineering.

A light matter, this, altogether? And yet an organic architecture must take this course and belie nothing, shirk nothing. Discipline! The architect who undertakes his work seriously on these lines is emancipated and imprisoned at the same time. His work may be severe, it cannot be foolish. It may lack grace; it cannot lack fitness altogether. It may seem ugly; it will not be false. No wonder, however, that the practice of architecture in this sense is the height of ambition and the depth of poverty!

Nothing is more difficult to achieve than the integral simplicity of organic nature, amid the tangled confusions of the innumerable relics of form that encumber life for us. To achieve it in any degree means a serious devotion to the "underneath" in an attempt to grasp the nature of building a beautiful building beautifully, as organically true in itself, and to its purpose, as any tree or flower. That is the need, and the need is demoralized, not served, by the same superficial emulation of the letter in the new work that has heretofore characterized the performances of those who start out to practice architecture by selecting to work in a readymade "style".

IN THE CAUSE OF ARCHITECTURE
☐ ☐ BY FRANK LLOYD WRICHT ☐ ☐

THE THIRD DIMENSION.   1925

Twenty-seven years ago a Society of arts and Crafts
was projected at Hull House in Chicago. The usual
artist disciples of Morris and Ruskin, devoted to making
things by hand, and a professorial element from the
University were assembled. Miss Jane Adams, the founder of Hull House, had invited me to be present and
toward the end of the enthusiastic meeting asked me
to contribute to the discussion. I had then been practicing Architecture for some years and I knew what I
had to say would be unwelcome: — so begged leave to
present my project in writing at the next meeting. I prepared the "Art and Craft of the Machine" which I then
delivered, advocating the patient study of the Machine
at work as the first duty of the modern artist. I had

invited to be present at the meeting, sheet metal workers, terra-cotta manufactures, tile and marble workers,
iron workers, wood workers, who were actually turning
out the work that was architectural Chicago, therefore
the architectural heart of America. The thesis I presented, simply stated, was — that the old ideals that had
well served the handicraft of old were now prostituted
to the machine — which could only abuse and wreck
them, that the world needed a new ideal recognizing
the nature and capability of the machine as a tool and
one that would give it work to do that it could do well, —
before any integrity could characterize our Art. I named
many things which I had found the machines then in
use in the trades could already do better than it had
ever been possible to do them by hand, — instancing
the emancipation from the old structural necessities
that the machine, as an artist's tool, had already brought
about. Finally I proposed that the society be formed to
intimately study the Machine's possibilities as a tool in
the hand of the artist, to bring it into the service of the

Beautiful — instead of serving as then and now — to destroy it.

Several brilliant disciples of Ruskin and Morris from the University of Chicago swept my propositions aside in a flood of sentimental eloquence: — I was voted down and out by the enthusiastic disciples of Ruskin and Morris, (whose sacred memory, it seems, I had profaned), and the Society was formed upon the same old basis of pounding ones fingers making useless things, that had been the basis of countless other "Art Societies" that had come to nothing in the end. So, together with my small band of modern industrials, I withdrew.

The Society as it was formed was a two-dimension affair that might foster Art as a pleasant amateur accomplishment, a superficial matter. It had rejected the third dimension, — the integral element, — on suspicion.

The machine as an Artist's tool — as a means to a great end in Art — did not exist for Ruskin and Morris, nor for the academic thought of that day.

Nor did the disciples of Ruskin and Morris, nor the architects and artists present at that much later date,

see it then. They do not see it yet and that is, very largely, what is the matter with Artist and with the Art, that is also craft, today.

The old structural necessity in Archictecture is dead. The Machine has taken it upon itself and "the raison d'etre" of the forms that were Architecture has therefore been taken away from them.

As the skeleton of the human figure is clothed with tissue in plastic sense to give us the human form, so the machine has made possible expressive effects as plastic in the whole — as is the human figure as an idea of form.

In all the crafts the nature of materials is emancipated by the Machine and the artist is freed from bondage to the old post-and-lintel form, the pilaster and architrave are senseless and Architecture in superimposed layers is now an "imposition" in every sense.

A modern building may reasonably be a plastic whole — an integral matter of three dimensions: a child of the imagination more free than of yore, owing nothing to "orders" or "styles".

Long ago both "orders" and "styles" became empty rituals — they were never Architecture — they were merely forms cast upon the shores of time by the Spirit of Architecture in passing. Architecture is the living-spirit of building truly and beautifully.

So the ground for a new life of Architecture of the third dimension, — an integral Architecture, — is furrowed thus by the machine and still fallow awaits the seed of common sense to germinate and grow in it, great true forms, — a vital living Architecture.

But like all simple things — too common to be interesting, too hard work to be attractive, the mastery of the machine is still to come, and a harsh ugliness, in relentless cruelty, obscures the common good.

The principle of the machine is the very principle of Civilization itself now focused in mechanical forms. Servants of brass and steel, and mechanical systems construct Civilization's very form today!

We have, whether we like it or not, here introduced an element into human life that is mastering the drudgery of the world, widening the margin of humain leisure. If dominated by human greed it is an engine of enslavement; — if mastered by the artist it is an emancipator of human possibilities in creating the Beautiful.

Yet the Machine is forced to mutilate and destroy old ideals instead of serving new ones suited to its nature — and because artists are become mere fashionable accidents or social indiscretions instead of masters, civilization is forced to masquerade in forms of "Art" false a century ago; the architectural "Renaissance" a sun still setting, — mistaken still for sun-rise.

To face simple truth seems too fearful a thing for those now claiming the title and place of the "artist." The simpletons hug their fond prejudices and predilections in foolish attempts to make them by book or hook or crook into queer little fashionable lies or gorgeous shams, so satisfied with results that any sane and sensible treatment of a project according to its nature is laughed at by and large — dubbed a freak and shown the door. Architecture in the hands of "Architects" has become a meaningless imitation of the less important aspect of the real thing: a mean form of bad surface decoration.

It is Engineering that now builds.

Until the spirit of this modern Engineering finds expression as integral decoration, which is the third dimension coming into play, Architecture does not live at all. The tools that produce work — (and by tools industrial systems and elements are also meant) — are now asked to do work to which they are wholly unsuited — "Styles" of work that were originated by hand when stone was piled on stone, and ornament was skillfully wrought upon it with clever human fingers: forms that were pruduced by a sensate power. Much as we may love the qualities of beauty then natural to such use and wont — we must go forward to the larger unity, the plastic sense of the "altogether" that must now be knowledge where then it was but instinct. The haphazard and picturesque must give way to ordered beauty emancipated from human fingers — living solely by human imagination controling, directing great co-ordinations of insensate power into a sentient whole. Standardization and repetition realized and beautified as a service rendered by

the Machine, and not as a curse upon the civilization that is irretrievably committed to it.

I am not sure that the Artist in this modern sense will be much like the picturesque personality of yore — in love with himself. Perhaps the quality in this modern will take off the curls and flapping hat of that love and show himself as sterner stuff in most umpopular guise. Nor will he be a "business man". The reward of exploitation he will not have. His task will be otherwise and elsewhere, — in the shops, — in the factories, with the industrial elements of his age, — as William Morris tried to be with them and for them; hot with face turned backward to the Medieval world, as his was, but forward to a new one — yet unseen.

In that new world, — all the resources that have accumulated to man's credit as the Beautiful will only be useful in the Spirit in which they were created and as they stood when they were original and true forms. The Renaissance in Architecture was always false except that the admixture of ideals and races necessarily confused

origins and so stultified them.

And finally there is seen in America the logical conclusion of the ideal of "re-hash" underlying the European Renaissance, a mongrel admixture of all the styles of all the world. Here in the United States may be seen the final Usonian degradation of that ideal — ripening by means of the Machine for destruction by the Machine. The very facility with which the "old orders of Beauty" are now become ubiquitous hastens the end. Academic thought and educational practices in America, seemingly, do not realize that the greatest of modern opportunities is being laid waste for the lack of that inner-experience which is revelation in the Soul of the Artist-mind; that sense of the third dimension as an essential factor to direct and shape the vital energy of these vast resources with integral forms if they are ever to have any spiritual significance at all: — if America is ever to really live.

And I know that America is a state of mind not confined to this continent — but awakening over the whole civilized world.

America by virtue of her youth and opportunity is logical leader — were she not swamped by European back-wash, — sunk in the "get culture quick" endeavor of a thoughtless, too-well-to-do new country like this, — buying its culture ready-made, wearing it like so much fashionable clothing, never troubled by incongruity or ever seeking inner significance.

A questionable bargain in the Antique, this culture, — knocked down to the highest bidder, for cash.

Through this self-satisfied, up-start masquerade — with its smart attitude and smug sensibilities, — this facetious parasite, skeptical of all save Fashion, this custom-monger whose very "life", as it sees it, would be taken by Truth — the new ideal must little by little work its way upward.

Among every hundred thousand opportunities, in the commercial sense, sacrificed to Fashion and Sham, — we may hope for one, sincerely groping for reality, one willing to run the gauntlet of ridicule in a great cause; one to risk the next "job" in single minded devotion to the one in hand, — or for that matter all that might come

BIRDS EYE VIEW OF GRANGE FOR
A W CUTTEN
FRANK LLOYD WRIGHT ARCHITECT

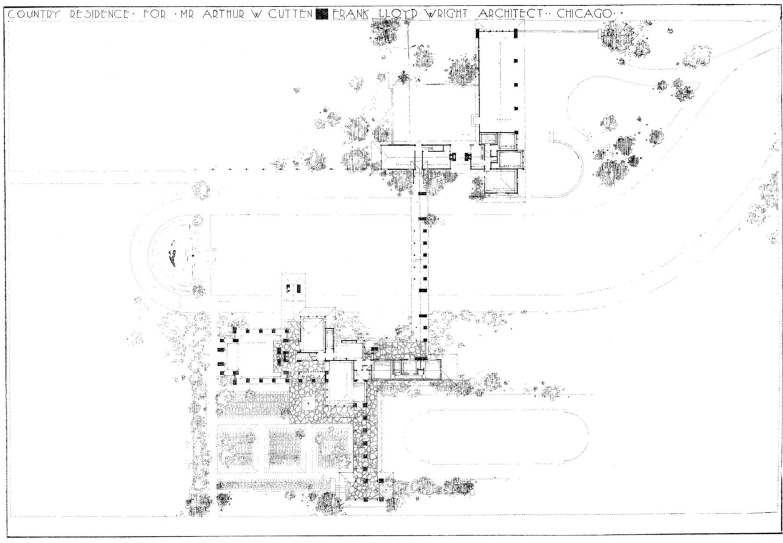

COUNTRY RESIDENCE · FOR · MR ARTHUR W CUTTEN ▪ FRANK LLOYD WRIGHT ARCHITECT · CHICAGO ·

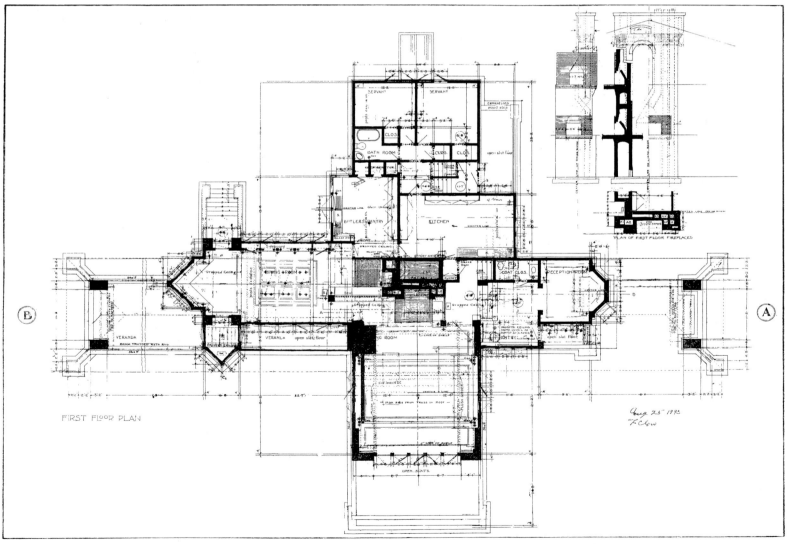

FIRST FLOOR PLAN

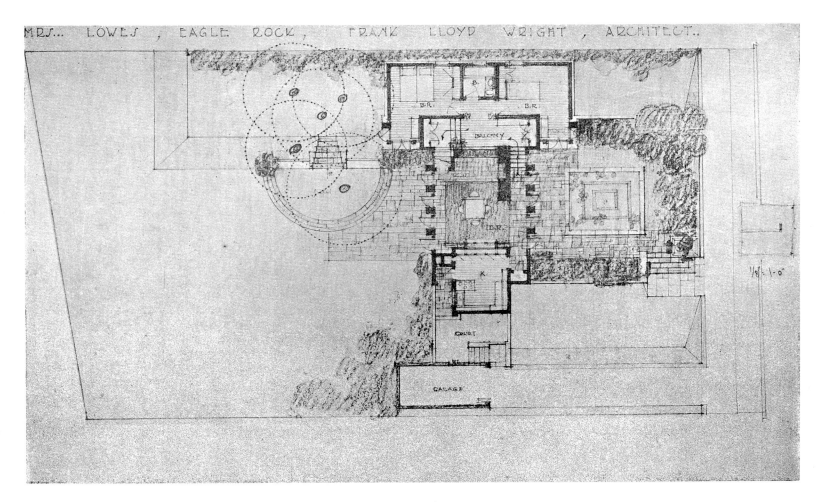

MRS. LOWES, EAGLE ROCK, FRANK LLOYD WRIGHT, ARCHITECT.

after, — for the precious sense of devotion to the freedom of Truth in creative work.

All that the new order signifies will not yet be found perfectly demonstrated in any one building. Each of the more sentient efforts will have a suggestion of it — a rare one may prophecy certain qualities to come in attributes already manifest: — the seed time is now but the harvest shall not be yet.

First, we shall see a process of simplification — a rejection of the old meaningless forms — an erasure of the laborious mess of detail now striving, sweating for "effect". We will have a clean line, a flat surface, a simply defined mass — to begin with. What a rubbish heap will be behind this effort when it is got well under way!

Again to life will be called a sense of materials used for their own sake: — their properties of line, form and color revealed in treatments that aim to bring them out in designs that employ their beauty as a fair means, truthful in a consistent whole. Columns, lintels, voussouirs, pilaster, architrave, capital and cornices — the whole grammer of the Art of building fashioned when the handicraft that imposed layer on layer in the old structural sense made it a fine thing — now false — inutile: the spirit of the old gone forward, — made free.

Form, in the new plastic sense, is now infinitely more elastic. The third dimension enters with the "plastic" ideal as the very condition of its existence. Realizism, as the outside aspect, is inutile. The abstraction that is the "within" is now reached.

Steel framing contributes a skeleton to be clothed with living flesh; reinforced concrete contributes the splay and cantilever and the continuous slab. These are several of the new elements in building which afford boundless new expressions in Architecture, as free, compared with post and lintel, as a winged bird compared to a tortoise, or an aeroplane compared with a truck.

The plastic order brings a sense of a larger unity in the whole, — and fewer parts —; monoliths where once we were content with patched and petty aggregates; soaring heights and sweeping breadths of line and mass uninterupted by niggling handicraft units, as the laboriously made aggregation in two dimensions gives way to the unity born of conditions — plastic now — the third dimension essential to its reality.

The Larkin Building, like all the work I have done, is an essay in the third dimension, a conservative recognition of the element of the Machine in modern life. In it the old order has been rejected that the Principle of Architecture may live anew. The building expresses the interieur as a singlè great vorm.

Unity Temple asserts again the quality and value of the third dimension in asserting the vorm within to be the essential to find expression. The reinforced concrete slab as a new architectural expression, is here used for its own sake as "Architecture". This building is a cast monolith. A transition building it is, wherein the character of the wooden forms or boxes, necessary at this time in casting concrete construction are made

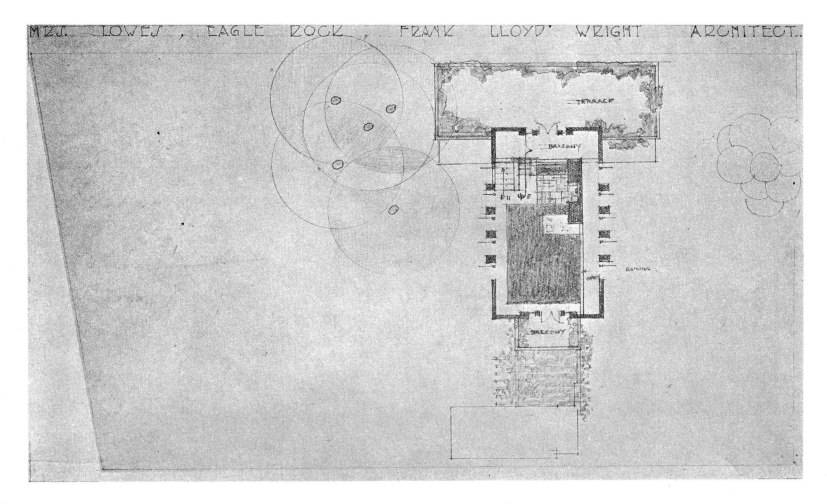

MRS. LOWES , EAGLE ROCK , FRANK LLOYD WRIGHT ARCHITECT.

a virtue of the whole in "style": that process of construction made a conscious aesthetic feature of the whole. Its "style" is due to the way it was "made". A sense of the third dimension in the use of the "box" and the "slab" — and a sense of the room within as the thing to be expressed in arranging them are what made Unity Temple; instead of the two-dimension-sense of the traditional block mass sculptured into architectural form from without.

The Coonley House at Riverside is of a type employing simple individual units, adapted each to its separate purpose, finally grouped together in a harmonious whole — simple materials revealed in its construction. The style of the Coonley Home is due to this simple use of materials with a sense of the human figure in scale, the prairie as an influence, — and a sense of the horizontal line as the line of domesticity: This home and all its relatives grows as a part of its site. It grows from it and is incorporated with it, not planted on it. And this sense of the indigenous thing, — a matter of the third-dimension, is a first condition of any successful treatment of any problem in the modern sense — as it was the secret of success in all great old work whereever it may be found, sub-concious then. But it must be used conciously now as a well defined principle. Any building should arise from its site as an expressive feature of that site and not appear to have descended upon it — or seem to be a "deciduous" feature of it. This "third-dimension" element in architecture made more concrete when the work of Art is regarded as

a plastic thing modeled as a fluid flowing, whole, as contrasted with the ideal of superimposition or aggregation or composition in the old structural sense, which was largely a two dimension affair. Nolonger may we speak of "composition".

Plastic treatments are always out of the thing, never something put on it. The quality of the third-dimension is found in this sense of depth that enters into the thing to develop it into an expression of it's nature.

In this architecture of the third-dimension "plastic" effects are usually produced from this sense of the within. The process of expression is development, proceeding from generals to particulars. The process never begins with a particular preconceived detail or silhouette to secure which the whole is subsequently built up. In such two-dimensional mental processes the sense of third dimension is wholly absent and not a natural thing but an applied thing is the inevitable result.

All the buildings I have built — large and small — are fabricated upon a unit system — as the pile of a rug is stitched into the warp. Thus each structure is an ordered fabric; — Rythm and consistent scale of parts and economy of construction are greatly facilitated by this simple expedient: — a mechanical one, absorbed in a final result to which it has given more consistent texture, a more tenuous quality as a whole.

I have wanted to build industrial Buildings in America but unfortunately, though trained as an engineer and in commercial building, I have become known as an artist-

Architect, the term Artist being one of reproach in my country, and therefore for the moment shunned in the commercial field.

While I should have preferred to be employed in this field at home I have been, for five years, constructing in a foreign country a romantic epic building, an architect's tribute to a uniqe nation he has much loved. This structure is not a Japanese building — nor an American building in Tokio. It is simply a free interpretation of the Oriental spirit, once more employing the old handicraft system and materials to create a rugged vital monolithic building that would help Japan to create the necessary new forms for the new life that is her choice and inevitable to her now. I felt it desirable to do this without out — raging all the noble Traditions which made that civilization a remarkable and precious thing in its own time.

But as a concession to the new spirit, the lava in this building and the brick are not used as structural materials. They are used as plastic covering "forms" cast in with the whole structure in decorative masses for their own sake. Where post and lintel construction is

resembled it is a mere coincidence of not importance enough to be avoided.

The Olive Hill work in Los Angelos is a new type in California, a land of romance, — a land that, as yet has no characteristic building material and no type of building except one carried there by Spanish missionaries in early days, a version of the Italian church and convent, — now foolishly regarded as an architectural "Tradition". I feel in the silhouette of the Olive Hill house a sense of the romance of the region when sens associated with its background and in the type as a whole a thing adaptable to California conditions. His type may be made from the gravel of decayed granite of the hills easily obtained there and mixed with cement and cast in molds or forms to make a fairly solid mass either used as blocks to compose a "unit-slab" sytem or monolithic in construction. This is the beginning of a constructive etfort to produce a type that would fully utilize standardization and the repetition of easily man-handled units. One of the essential values of the service rendered by the Machine, as elements in an architecture modeled by the "third-dimension" is this standardizing

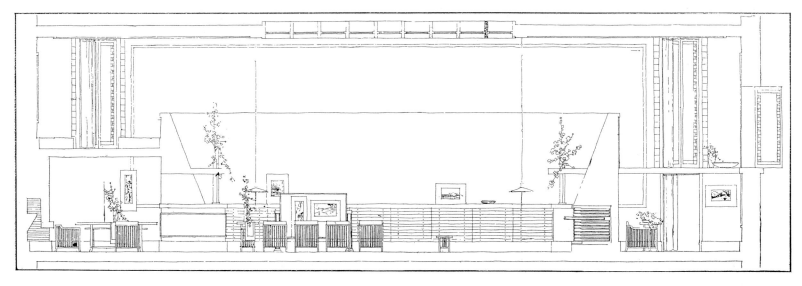

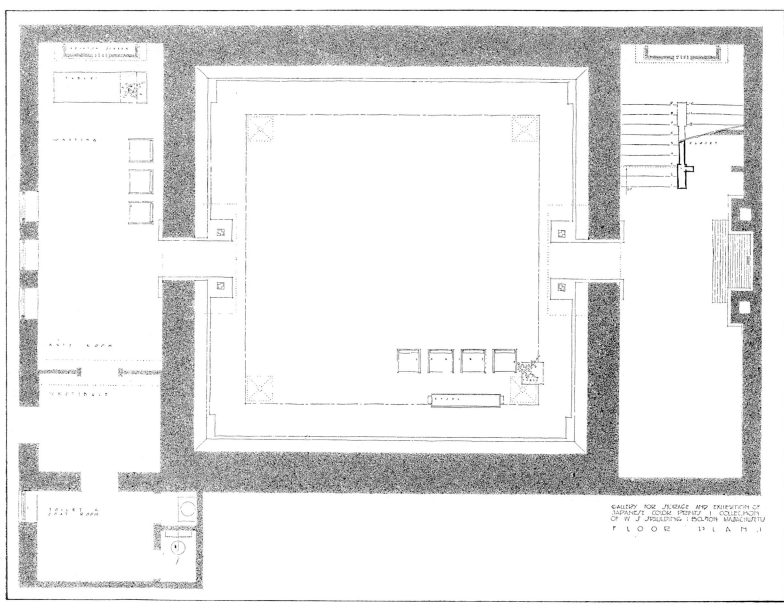

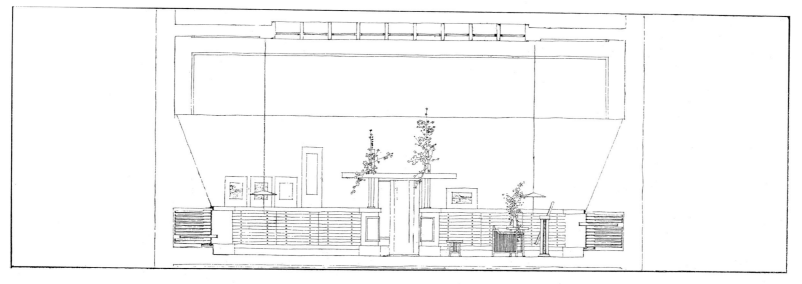

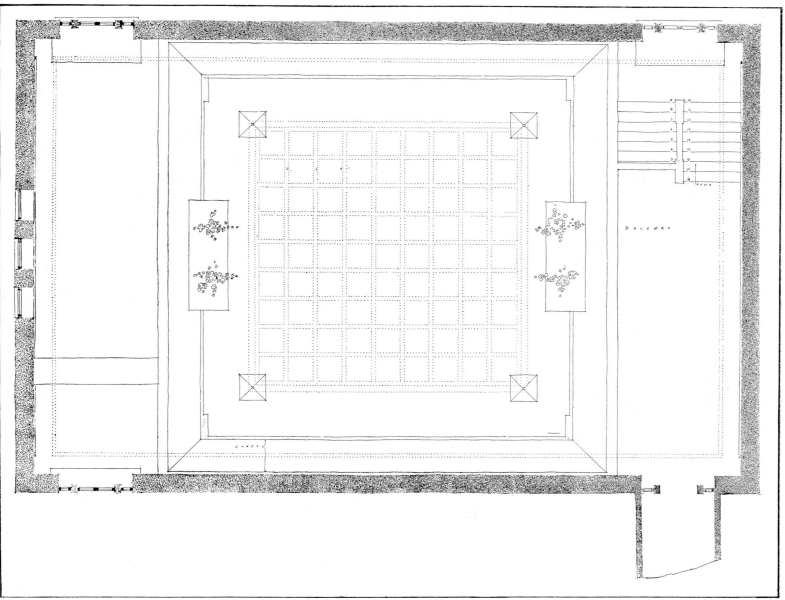

of a convenient unit for structural purposes. I am still engaged in this effort.

It is a mistaken notion that the legitimate use of the Machine precludes ornamentation. The contrary is the case. Pattern, — the impress of the imagination, — is more vital than it ever was in the use of any other system or "tool" in any other age. But before we can find the significant expressions that give poetry and endless variety to this new architecture in any integral sense we shall first have protested the old "ornamentation" by reverting to clean forms expressive as such in themselves. Little by little, the use of significant virile pattern will creep in to differentiate, explain and qualify as a property of the third dimension

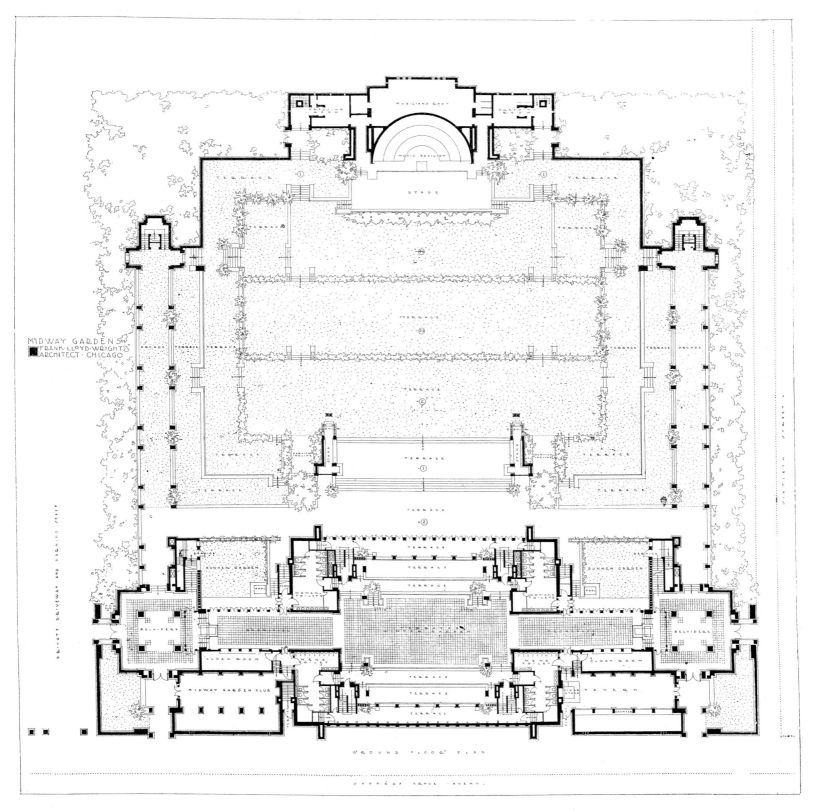

MIDWAY GARDENS
FRANK·LLOYD·WRIGHT
ARCHITECT·CHICAGO

as poetry. And the materials and structural enclosures will ever be increasing thereby in significance and what we call beauty. Imagination will vivify the background and expression of modern life, as truly and more universally and richly than was ever before seen in the world, — even in the aesthetic background of the Moors or the Chinese.

The sneer of "factory aesthetics" goes by its mark.

It is the Imagination that is new challenged, not the Memory.

When the industrial building of a country are natural buildings, and vital expressions of the conditions under-

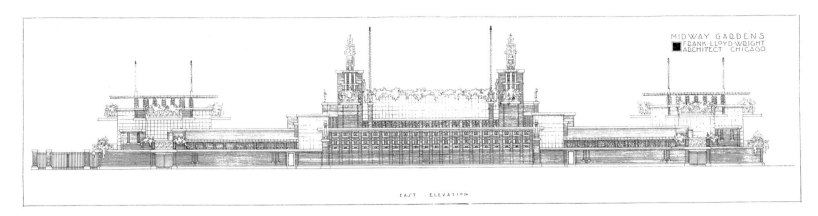

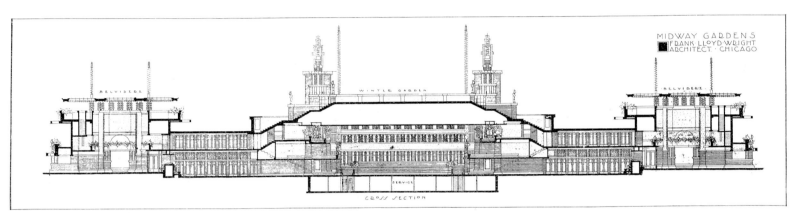

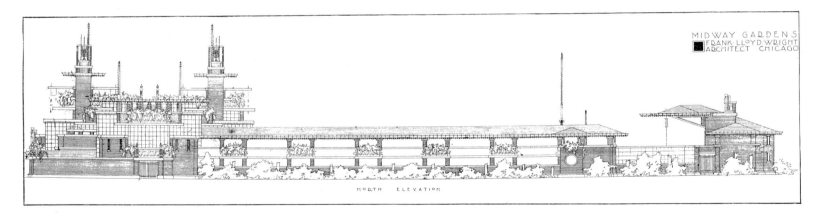

lying their existence — the domestic architecture of that country will be likewise true; a natural, indigenous expression of modern life in its broader aspects and finer opportunities. This natural expression must be conditioned upon service rendered by the Machine, — the Machine bringing man the fruits, that in olden times belonged only to the mastering few — to belong now to the many. In this we see the Machine the forerunner of Democracy.

Buth then the machine will not be, as now, engaged in impartially distributing meretricious finery of a bygone age, senselessly, from avenue to alley, — but, as that "finery" was once really fine, — so again fullness and richness of life fitted to purpose in infinite poetic variety shall come to us.

Beauty may come abide with us in more intimate spirit than ever graced and enriched the lives of the mas-

terful-few in the ancient "Glory that was Greece" or the "Grandeur that was Rome" if we master the Machine in this integral sense. It is time we realized that Grecian buildings have been universally overrated as Architecture: They are full of lies, pretence and stupidity. And the Roman architecture, but for the nobility of the structural arch, a thing now dead, — was a wholly debased version of the better Greek elements that preceded it. Both civilizations have been saddled upon us as the very ideal so long that our capacity to think for ourselves is atrophied. Yet, we may now, from the vision opened by the ideal of a plastic architecture, look down upon the limitations of this antique world with less respect and no regret. We have wings where they had only feet, usually in leaden shoes. We may soar in individual freedom of expression where they were wont to crawl — and we are the many where they were the

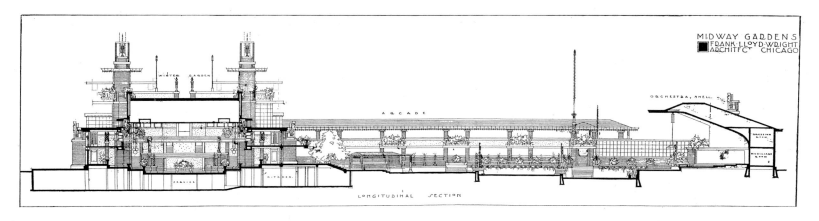

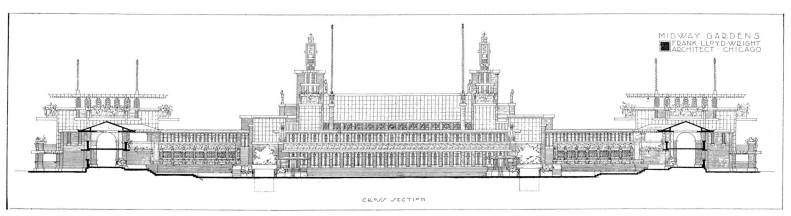

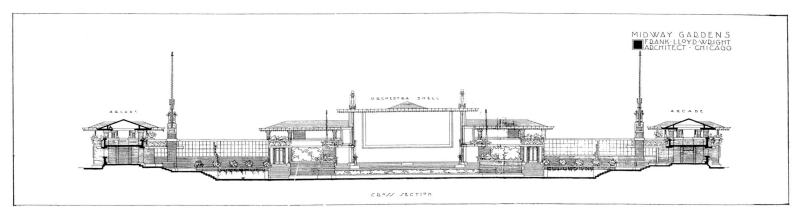

few. A superior breath and beauty in unity and variety is a universal possibility to us — if we master the Machine and are not, as now, mastered by it.

In the modern Machine we have built up a monster image of ourselves that will eventually destroy us unless we conquer it — and turn it from its work of enslavement to its proper and ordained work of emancipation. Then, in its proper place, — the margin of human leisure inmeasurably widened, — the plastic in Art become a free flowing channel for imaginative creative effort, we will have a background for life that is integral — a setting incomparably more organic and expressively beautiful as a whole than has ever been known before in the world — and more than that, an expression in itself of the best ideals, the purest sentiment for the beauty of Truth in all forms of life — ever yet realized by Man.
□ □ □ □

THE SOCIAL BACK GROUND OF FRANK LLOYD WRIGHT
□ □ BY LEVIS MUMFORD □ □

The art of our time differs from that of earlier periods in that the best of it is usually produced without a "destination". Since the original artist is no longer in harmony with the community from which he must draw his patrons, he must count his audience among posterity; and in order to assure this we have created the anomalous esthetic temple called the museum. What is true of sculpture and painting is likewise true of architecture; with this unfortunate difference — that the museum is of no use to the architect, and that the needs and ideals of posterity will doubtless change to such an extent that the best modern buildings, lucky enough

to survive the depredations of the ground-landlord and the financier, will have only an historical interest; they will serve, in other words, as models for the kind of revivalist who now goes back to Le Nôtre or Adam or the medieval builders:

I have stated the bare paradox; let me now correct it. The architect of the last fifty years has been faced with a host of new problems, anyone of which — the use of steel and glass, for example — was sufficiently big to have exhausted the efforts of a whole generation. He faced these problems in a period that had ceased to be unified in its ideas or direct and simple in its technical methods; and except for certain regions where the Renaissance tradition maintained a sort of fossilized strength, the architect's technical solutions were baffled and obscured by waves of "style," on which one or another revival would ride. For the great body of architects only two paths lay open: they could concentrate upon "style," upon the expressional elements of building, and associate their names with the manipulation and restatement of some established mode; or they could put questions of esthetic expression into a minor place, and expend all their skill in dealing with the technical processes.

In America, these alternatives were carried to their respective extremes. On one hand, a group of cultivated architects, headed by Messrs. White and McKim, turned their backs on the vulgarities of construction and consented to use their talents only on buildings where they had a free hand with the program. Their attitude turned them naturally to mansions, clubs, churches, and public institutes, where the historic connection with the past was obvious, where the utilitarian requirements had been pretty well explored, where, in short, the technical means could be subordinated, even at some slight inconvenience to the occupants, to pure form. Whether this group of architects conceived their forms as classic, as gothic, or as renaissance, they did little to expand the meanings of these terms; they refined, they simplified, they became infinitely exact in syntax and grammatical construction; worst of all, they committed no mistakes! Their esthetic solutions were as impeccable as the morals of an Egyptian mummy; and for the same reason: they were dead!

What happened to the other architects? Well, they turned to the difficult problems of engineering: they created hospitals in which every surgical and medical requirement had been planned with exactitude, schools in

which the rooms never became stuffy or dank towards the end of the day, hotels in which food could be served, hot, in half a dozen great rooms to unexpected numbers of guests, and homes in which the drudgeries of menial service were reduced to a minimum. Perhaps the best American architects, particularly during the last twenty years, have belonged to this second school: they have been primarily technicians and engineers, and although they have paid a respectful homage to Art, they have never let it stand in the way of what they and their clients look upon as more practical and important matters. "Style" in the sense that the first group used the term did indeed too often remain as an esthetic appendage upon their rigorous and logical work: but it was usually the insincere tribute of men not sufficiently confident in their powers, and not sufficiently awakened to modern art, to realize that the design and ornament of the present age can necessarily have nothing to do with the eggs and darts, the gargoyles and ribbed vaulting, in short, with the icecream forms and the pastrycook esthetics which symbolize the "style" of the stylicists. Outside these two schools in America have stood a handful of men. After the Civil war, the great figure of H. H. Richardson bestrode our buildings, and for a while

it seemed as if he might give a complete solution to the double problem of function and expression. It was his misfortune, however, to base his architecture upon masonry forms, the bulkiest and sturdiest masonry that has ever appeared in America; and so, though he designed railway stations and office buildings, and made sketches of grain elevators and ice-houses, he was eclipsed in the decade that followed through the rise of new modes of construction and only a few young men remained to carry on, in the spirit, the Richardson tradition. One of these men was the late Louis Sullivan, who was perhaps the first to find the logical form for steel cage construction; another was Mr. Frank Lloyd Wright. With all the differences that characterize the work of the two older men, they were in search, as Louis Sullivan said in The Autobiography of an Idea, of a rule so broad as to admit no exceptions; and it is in this sense that Mr. Wright, I believe, carries on and pushes further the work of his forerunners.

With the immense amount of construction that goes on in our community, how is it that these initiatives seem as solitary as they are significant? In order to understand this, we must go back a generation in American life.

Frank Lloyd Wright is an original artist; and roughly, after 1890 the American business man, the Lorenzos and Fuggers and Louis's of our imperial and financial order, became afraid of original art. I hasten to explain that this had not always been the case. Between 1840 and 1880 was the halcyon period of originality in America: the greatest praise that could be applied to a building was the assertion that it was unique. During that period the American was completely contemptuous of European art: the contempt, unhappily, was based upon ignorance, upon a belief in industrial ugliness for its own sake, and upon a conviction that high art and republican institutions automatically flourished together. It followed that the past in Europe had nothing to offer which the present in America could not produce — and produce bigger, better, more quickly: The cultural churlishness of the American of that period is best expressed, perhaps, in Mark Twain's Innocents Abroad: it had its counterpart in an architecture which, though full of unconscious tags from the past, was like nothing the world had ever seen before. It was modern; it used machine-carved ornament and metallic constructions; and, incidentally, it was uniquely hideous. Such archi-

tecture was not altogether unknown in Europe, perhaps, during this period; but intelligent people were not inclined to boast about it.

Sometime in the nineties, it would seem, the American replaced his complacent ignorance of historic art with an equally absurd and servile respect. The cultural humility which Henry James pictured in The Americans broke out into an ostentatious effort to appear at home and at ease amid the great art and culture of the past; the architect's patron became conscious of the fact that the creations of an earlier age not merely proclaimed his bad taste but the newness of his suddenly-arrived riches. So he patronized the architect who followed precedent, and who thus threw a veil of decent antiquity around a social position achieved only yesterday. "Safety first" is an American phrase; and safety first became the ruling word in architecture. A good building became one which in almost every particular was based upon some acknowledged old building. The desire to possess "old masters" did not confine itself to pictures; for the pictures needed a frame, and it remained for the architect to supply one. This panic for esthetic security extended itself even to buildings which were

palpably designed for use; hence early skyscrapers with Renaissance facades, like the universally known Flatiron building; hence later ones with putative medieval ornament like the Woolworth Tower and the Bush Tower — the Bush Tower which but for a perverse stylicism might indeed have been a beautiful building. What was the original architect to do in such a situation? Fortunately, there is never a large supply of original artists; so the great mass of the profession complacently followed one of the two paths I have indicated; and those who did not, preserved their integrity and individuality only by forfeiting a large part of the opportunities that their talents would normally have earned, had they been more amenable to popular needs and snobbish desires. The center of American architecture has been occupied by the able technicians: the periphery has been divided between the cultivated stylicists and the outcaste, who were neither fashionable, nor in a narrow sense "practical". In a sense, Mr. Wright is our most distinguished outcast. It is no little honor.

Frank Lloyd Wright's work, as I see it, is an attempt to apply the logic of the machine to humane building. His architectural conceptions are far removed from the conservative architects who will not carry modern pro-cesses to their inevitable conclusions; they are equally removed from the notions advocated by architects like Le Corbusier who are not essentially concerned with humane building, and would be quite pleased to remodel our whole environment in accordance with the narrow physical processes that are served in the factory. That the old principles of masonry construction are not sufficient in an age that uses steel and so can, within limits, prolong its horizontals, is of course plain; that the old systems of decoration and ornament should no more survive in buildings than the false classicism of the academies should survive in the studios, is likewise plain: at any rate these things are plain to those who are not trying to bolster up some special interest in the academies. Once these things are granted, however, the lines of departure are many; and although the ignorant like to lump the modernists in a single group, we shall presently realize, I trust, that the modernism of Mr. Frank Lloyd Wright places him among the new poets and artists, whereas the modernism of l'Esprit Nouveau is but a continuation of an acerbic puritan philosophy that has degraded life and art throughout the whole period of the industrial transition. In short, among the modernists we have the school which would make the

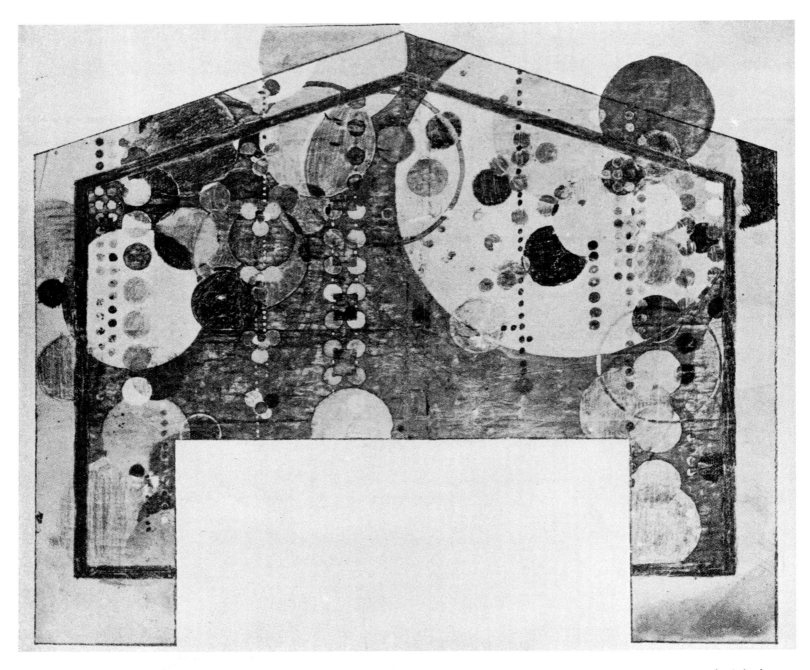

machine and machine-principles dominant; and the school which would take possession of the machine, modify it, renold it, humanize it, restoring man to the central position which the "advance" of the last two hundred years has undermined. Am I wrong in holding that Mr. Wright's work stands for this second tendency? If so, it is not merely an accomplishment: it is also a prophecy, or at least an hypothesis; and to the extent that we transform and humanize our current institutions, we may expect to see more or less of Mr. Wright's kind of architecture.

Esthetically speaking, what has been Mr. Wright's achievement? He has taken advantage of the wide freedom offered by modern constructional forms, and of the great range of suggestions offered by engineering, to alter the conventional line, accent, and interval of our houses and buildings. Like every true architect he is a poet in space; and he cannot express what belongs peculiarly to our own generation in art without altering the windowheights, the openings, the depths that have become fixed in traditional architecture. There is a parallel between Mr. Frank Lloyd Wright's work and that of some of our modern poets in America: such a man, for example, is Carl Sandburg, Mr. Wright's fellow townsman in Chicago. Both of them have faced our age, have absorbed the broken rhythm of the machine, feel the jagged geometry of our new adventures in space: they have something to express in plastic or literary form that an earlier age was not aware of. Were they less sensitive to form, were they less deeply poetic, they would have nothing to say at all; they would become merely reporters or engineers. The point is that they have interposed themselves between our material activities and their own works, and in so doing have begun

to react upon their environment: so the cacophony of Chicago becomes a poem: so the relenless vigor of the machines becomes an expression of the human spirit, and Mr. Wright's houses become things with human associations, memories, prospects; in short, they are not merely endurable, as a sanitary tenement may be, but liveable, as someday the whole human hive may again become.

It is just because the best of Mr. Wright's work is prophetic that it necessarily stands outside our age; and seems foreign both to those who glory in machinery and those who cling pathetically to the cultural tags of other ages. Mr. Wright has had the great intuition to see that modern science and technology can be used and expressed without reducing every building to the common mathematical denominator of the factory; indeed, is not the persistent use of gardens, aquaria, and great pots of plants in Mr. Wright's designs an emblem of the fact that, unlike the mere mechanists, he recognizes the value of living processes, and places at the core of his architectural conception, not a machine, but that which lives and grows and reproduces and renews and makes the world gay? The world of current industry and business is not yet quite prepared to receive this revelation: it would be a disturbing, or rather, a devastating one; for, as Mr. G. K. Chesterton has well said, "there are financial combinations and imperial conquests and commercial cooperations on a huge scale that are every bit as barren and useless and unproductive as throwing a pebble into the sea;" and the architecture that exists merely to glorify these things is, as we say vulgarly in America, "off its base." For this reason, perhaps, Mr. Wright's work has mainly been confined to houses, hotels, amusements parks; in short to the

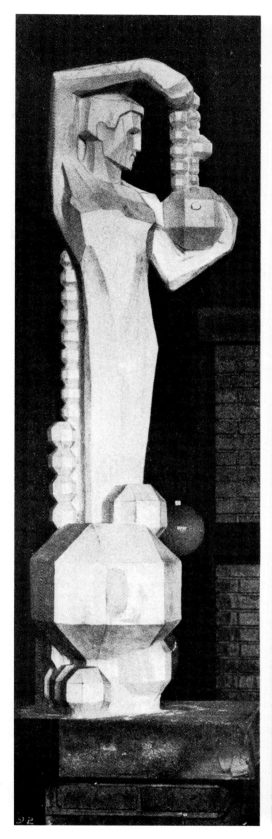
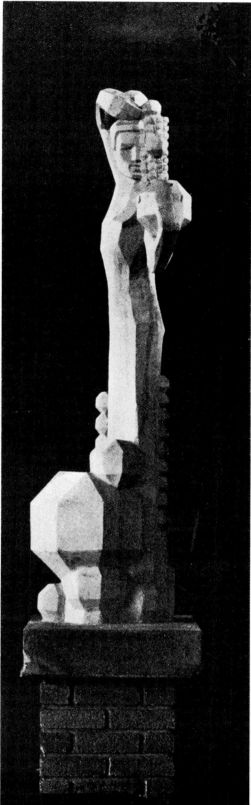

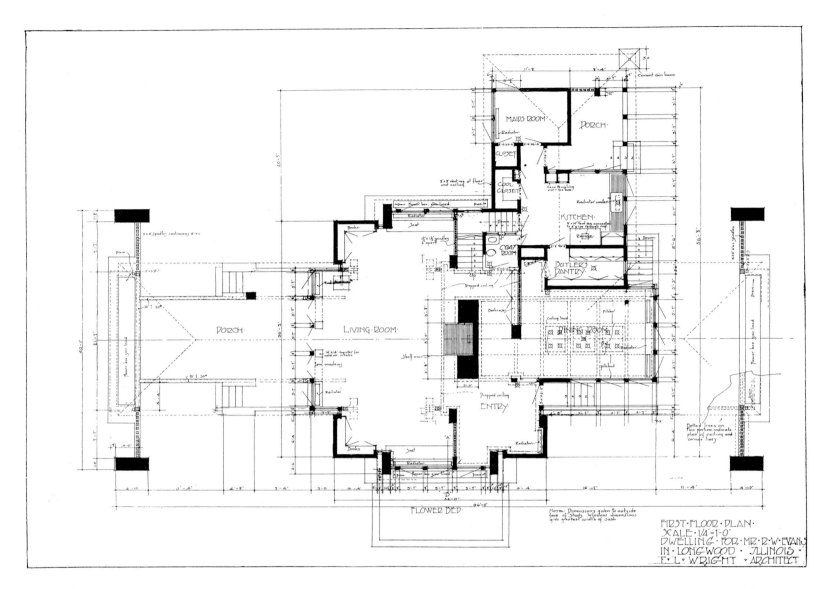

FIRST·FLOOR·PLAN·
SCALE·1/4"·=·1'-0"
DWELLING·FOR·MR·R·W·EVANS
IN·LONGWOOD·ILLINOIS·
F·L·WRIGHT·ARCHITECT

kind of building that functionally embodies the ideas for which Mr. Wright stands.

Finally, to what extent is Mr. Wright's architecture "American"? Those in Europe who admire Mr. Wright's work are particularly distressed by the fact that it has scarcely achieved a wide recognition in our own country. The explanation for this relative lack of influence lies partly in the conditions that I have been describing, partly in the fact that these new poetic forms demand a certain alteration of old habits and associations; partly also, no doubt, it is due to the fact that in working out his new rhythms Mr. Wright has refused to be confined to the ship-shape utilitarian demands of the ordinary house; hence the small builder, with limited means, does not find Mr. Wright's experiments easy models to follow. There is still another explanation; namely, that Mr. Wright's low-lying houses, with their flat roofs, which seem about to dissolve into the landscape, are an expression of the prairie: it is no accident that these forms have been so readily appreciated in the Netherlands and on the plains of Prussia. In other words, Mr. Wright has created a true regional form; and it is inevitable that this form should awaken deeper feelings of appreciation in similar regions than in parts of the same political unit that have a different reaction to the landscape. As a New Yorker, with a perpetual sense of the upward thrust of the Palisades, of the Westchester Hills, of the skyscraper, I feel a foreign element in Mr. Wright's work; for there are many Americas, and as we begin to settle down in our country we become conscious of subtleties and differences which, in the mere march across the continent, we neglected and ignored. Mid-American, and perhaps Mediterranean (Californian) Mr. Wright's architecture is: it is as mid-American as Sherwood Anderson's novels or Carl Sandburg's poems.

In conclusion. Science and poetry, knowledge and the humane arts, are divided in our own time as they were perhaps never divided before. To remedy this division, various people have suggested that we let science and technology take the place of all that our life now lacks, that we look to science and technology, not merely for means, but for values and norms. Most of those who hold out against this conception have an equally

sterile alternative: they think that we can continue to live by the fossilized values brought over from other ages. The task of the original artist today, and in essence it is the same in literature, in philosophy and in architecture, is to bring "science" and "poetry" together again, for the knowledge which brings only power is brutal, and the culture which isolates itself from the sources of power is futile. Mr. Wright's buildings, it seems to me, are essays towards this synthesis: if they are not completely successful, that merely shows that the difficulty which confronts us will require the work of a hundred Wright's. A logical architecture, skilled in the use of new processes and materials, expressive of new relationships in space, mass, line; capable of giving coherent form to every need and capability for which we need a physical shell, unified in conception, no matter what the particular plan or program — this is what our age needs. The architecture of Frank Lloyd Wright is inevitably only a beginning; but if I am not mistaken, it points in the right direction.

□   □   □   □

FRANK LLOYD WRIGHT □ BY DR. H. P. BERLAGE □

A period of quickly changing tendencies in art indicates a tottering principle of construction. Thus the strength of the individual who, as soon as he creates an independent form, is in the way of creating a school; which means that a strong personality obtains not only superficial followers — the admirers of the exterior revelation only — but also they who, in virtue of their talent, probe to the essence of the new form from the very start.
It is the fascination of the "new gift" which attracts, which, with one stroke stimulates change and propagates itself with inconceivable rapidity. It has the same effect as that of a stone thrown into a pond. A rapid transition of this kind is impossible where the changed view of art is of more general import, that is, when it is not the actual art-form that undergoes the change but when it is a question of a systematical change of principle; briefly, when personal originality makes room for collective universality.

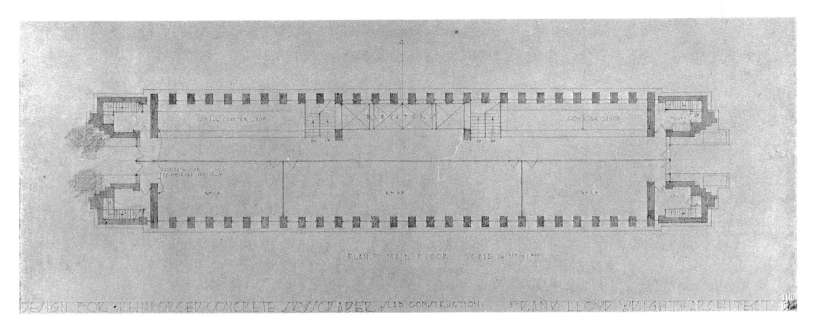

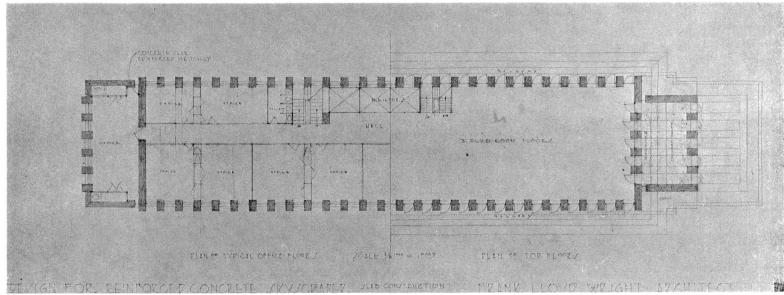

When some years ago, in my memoirs of my American travels, I gave my impression of Frank Lloyd Wright's work and, during a lecture, ventured to suggest that "peaceful American penetration" might one day occur as a reciprocal action to the preceding European movement, all I meant was that the work of that great architect would certainly not remain unnoticed in Europe; unless, by any chance, his work should be representative of general American architecture. And this especially as Wright, after Sullivan, his master, has entirely freed himself from European architecture.

When producing his work, Wright wrote an important study on style-copying, (so especially fatal for America) as a result of a revision of the great periods of art and the value of the various styles, which culminates in a hatred of Renaissance.

Now it is in this connection that I feel the great difficulty of determining the "cultural" significance of an artist in a time like the present, for one cannot escape the primary question as to whether his work represents a general rather than a particular value. And then I believe I must regard Wright's as typical of the latter and to honour him most as the endowed artist whose influence ought to be assured as a matter of course through his really "enchanting" gift. Now "to reveal the universal in the particular" is certainly the attribute of genius but the "universal" in question here has scarcely made a start on even the construction of the very latest skyscraper. For, although Wright has certainly created a centre of art of first importance for his country, yet the character of his art cannot be termed typically American. In that case, its character would bear a more mechanical stamp; a building by Wright would then have to be constructed with the inexorable rationalism of the machine, of which no single part is unaccounted for. And this "a priori", not meaning that the artist must necessarily degenerate into a mere machine but that he in any case becomes proof against romantic susceptibility.

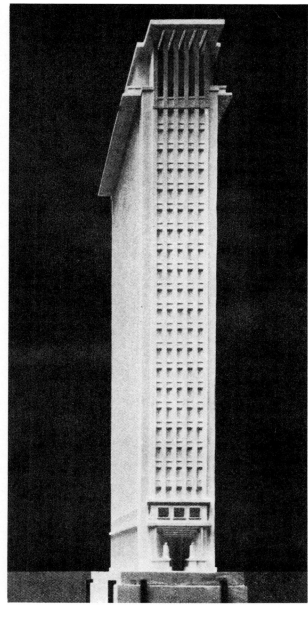

In any case, I find it difficult to see Wright otherwise than as a romanticist and to see him as his very antipode, that is, as an "industrial architect", as many like to see him — as he likes to see himself — witness a monograph from his pen "In the Cause of Architecture", in which he writes:

"I desire from a building the same as that which I demand of a human being, viz., that it be sincere and intrinsically true, to which principal virtue I wish to see added as much charm and lovableness as is conceivable. But intrinsic integrity is the essential. The machine is the tool peculiar to our age and it is therefore an important task to furnish this machine with work to which it is suited."

"The adaptation of work to its possibilities is the essence of the modern industrial ideal, which we shall have to build up if architecture is not to lose its leading place in art." This is where Wright proves that America's soil is most certainly expected to cradle true modern architecture —

which was held in contempt by the great pioneers of the English movement.

Further: "The constructive limitations are the artist's best friends. The machine will never more be banished from the world; it is and remains the pioneer of democracy, the ultimate aim of our hopes and wishes. The architect of our day should recognise no task more important than that of adapting this modern instrument, as far as such be at all possible. What does he do instead, however? He misuses this instrument in order to create forms which originated in a different time and under a different sky, forms which to day have a paralysing effect because there is no escape from them anywhere; and all this happens with the aid of the machine whose task it is, on the contrary, to destroy these forms." Wright wrote that in 1908, since when the old forms have not yet been completely abolished, at least certainly not in America. For even there, an art with a style borrowed from the machine (the which is different from

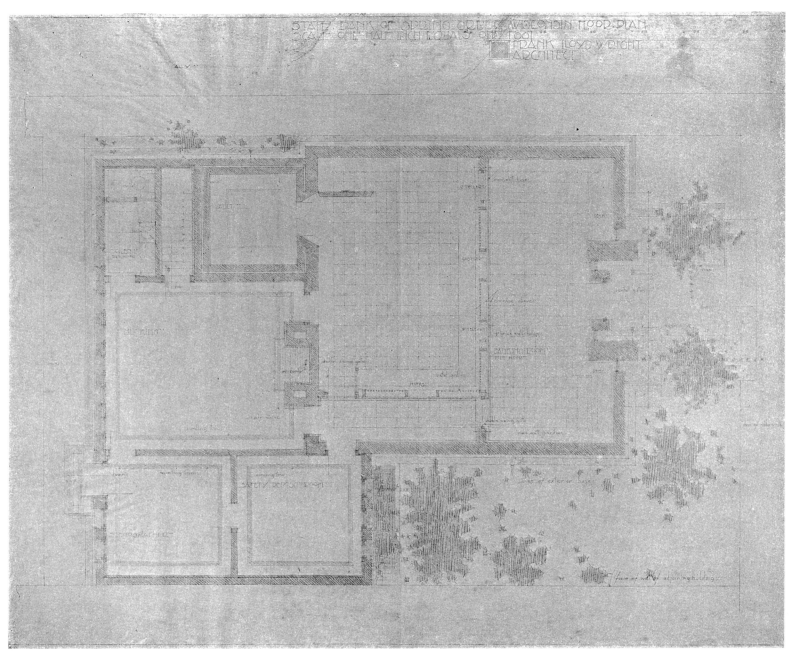

a mechanical manufacture of parts and no more) has as yet to be as good as entirely built up.

Now, does Wright's work answer to this ideal, formulated so precisely by himself? I hope I do the great American no injustice in denying it. Nor, when I saw the achieved work with my own eyes, did I receive the impression of an "universal art" of this kind but rather of a "personal", charming and lovable art, at the root of which the mechanical lies only apparently.

And how does this "personal" art reveal itself, at least in the country house, to which for the present Wright's principal activity has been mainly restricted?

In severe horizontalism, with a gabled ending to a closed row of small windows and which is characterised by an immensely projecting, slightly sloping roof.

For horizontalism, as such, is not proper only to Wright. This seems to be generally modern, probably explain-able as a reaction upon the after-effects of the verticalism of the neo-Gothic movement. It is also very distinctly discernible in the latest architecture of Amsterdam, pursued even in the arrangement of the window-panes. But that leap of the roof, with its tremendous shade effect, through which its protective function (never so prominent as with Wright) found expression, is and remains the find, the fascinating piquancy of the "tridimensional", as a pupil of Wright's characterised his work. That is why he, himself, becomes a slave to this motif, which becomes objectionable when used superfluously and especially in asymmetrical application. And this happens pretty frequently because the plans of those houses are adapted with marvellous perfection (to which symmetrical construction does not usually lend itself) to the most complete effect of the rooms in their relation to each other and in their con-

nection with the site.

In this arrangement of room, Wright is at his highest powers and, moreover, as a worshipper of Nature, calls in solely the living flower to his aid in his decorations. In their honour he constructs the long stone bowls under the windows, and round ones for gate-piers at the entrances or on the terraces. Inside, moreover, the consistent strength of his style, with its long, straight lines, especially in heavy ceiling construction, is in greatest evidence. For Wright refuses to recognise almost every curve, in spite of the fact that he occasionally makes use of the manifold recessed, half-circle arch for his entrances and, for his ceillings (and this I regard as a weakness), round-vaulting, as in his "Dana-Hause" at Spring-field. Moreover, the rooms are low and the wide-stretched, huge, brick fire place accentuates this character. Suitable boarding and the furniture, heavily and ration-

ally constructed, is like the European furniture of the beginning of the modern movement. Indeed, surprise upon surprise is met with in these rooms; when looking outside over the brightly coloured flower basement towards the landscape, as also when looking inside through the many, often doorless apertures (an American custom) to the adjoining corridors or rooms. And while looking, admiration increase sfor the poet of this poem of space because he has, moreover, exquisitely sensitive taste for placing all the objects of art, made for the pur pose, in the right place.

Although Wright's talent developed in building houses, the opportunity was given him to reveal his extraordinary art in the building of a church (Unity Church near Chicago) and an official building (the offices of the Larkin factories in Buffalo). For in that church — a rectangular building — something of the classical temple is

revived and the offices — in their brutal mass — display the unflinching strength of industrial life in these times. For the church he used the same motif as for the country houses — the high-placed row of windows with the projecting, but in this case flat roof. In the offices he departed from the motif, possibly considering it unsuited to the materialism of this factory office; for the character of this building, undoubtedly borrowed from his own, is more consistent than any other with that which Wright developed in his "programme of principles". The businesslike character is especially expressed in the tremendous interior space, formed into a working hall, where one greatly appreciates the fact that he decorated the upper gallery — the gallery of repose — with flowers and plants. For this reason it is to be hoped that Wright's field of activity will stretch still further in that direction; for in one of his last works — an hotel at Tokio — he evidently completes the apotheosis of what he realised in the country-house "Coonley". This hotel gave him an opportunity — partly because of its exceptional dimensions — to stretch his imagination to the utmost with this great chance for applying his characteristic motifs.

As a matter of fact, Wright's talent is extremely manysided. He has made "ideal projects", such as architects term those designs which are pre-destined never to be executed. I refer to a theatre in California of more classical conception with surroundings which were created for an architectural Eden. Then to "Olive Hill", a country house in that same wonderful country, this time executed, in which Eastern influences have been at work. Would not his stay in Japan be responsible for this? In my opinion, the architecture of a summer garden with an open-air theatre witnesses to it most pointedly. For in this garden, fantastic pales rise up, angularly grooved, and similar beams and chassis project, everything for the sake of effect that is certainly Japanese in character. And then there are all manner of figurative finishes which peculiarise the character. But does not the awning-shaped roof, itself, come from that same East? Admiration for Wright, therefore, is comprehensible and, in congruity with the fate of the prophets, I suppose, is more in evidence on this side of the Ocean than on the

other. Even our own country (Holland) where, at this moment, a modern national architecture is growing, has here and there been unable to escape this "foreign slur". But should one regard such a leader with a jealous eye? At all times and in every art development outside influences have been at work, according to circumstances of general as well as of a passing nature. In most cases it will probably be the latter because the actual art form changes more easily and, therefore, is more easily superseded.

Historically, the most striking example of this development, that of the Renaissance — be it moreover only the decorative character of this art — is explained.

The ultra individualism of the present times naturally increases this possibility considerably. But in any case, an influence of this kind proceeds from the very foremost only, and if it had not already been an established fact that Wright holds a place among the greatest architects of these times, then it could certainly be concluded from the influence he exercises.

□   □   □   □

THE INFLUENCE OF FRANK LLOYD WRIGHT ON THE ARCHITECTURE OF EUROPE □ □ BY J. J. P. OUD □ □

Although I am deeply convinced of the relativity of all appreciation in art, where contemporaries or persons very near to us are concerned, yet in my opinion the figure of Frank Lloyd Wright towers so assuredly above the surrounding world, that I make bold to call him one of the very greatest of this time without fearing that a later generation will have to reject this verdict.

Of such flawless work as his, appearing amidst architectural products which, in their lack of style, will have to be designated "nineteenth century style"; of such unity of conception in the whole and in details; of such a definite expression and straight line of development another example can hardly be given.

Whereas it is a peculiarity of our day, that even the work of the cleverest nearly always betrays h o w it grew to be such as it i s, with Wright everything i s, without

being at all perceptible any mental exertion to produce. Where others are admired for the talent with which we see them master their material, I revere Wright because the process by which his work came into being, remains for me a perfect mystery.

It is no detraction from this reverence, which retained its high degree through the varying phases of my own development, when, asked to give my views on the important, even great influence of Wright on European architecture, I do not call this influence a happy one in all respects.

What happened to that influence might be compared to what occurred with the rise of a "Wright-school" in the West of America. Concerning the latter Wright once wrote in a pessimistic mood, that he grieved to see that the form in which he had expressed his ideas in his works, appeared to have a greater attraction than those ideas themselves. Since those ideas aimed at starting from the function and not from the form, he believed this to be "pernicious" to the development of architecture in general.

Pernicious in that sense I would also call the sugges-

tive influence which the rare giftedness of Wright has exerted on the architecture this side the Atlantic. In the confusion of opinions which in the European architecture of the last decades — after the too great unanimity and certainty of former generations — raised each suggestion which was not too absurd all at once to an almost nerve-exhausting problem, the oeuvre of Wright, when it became more thoroughly known, could not fail to work as a revelation. Free from all finical detail-work, which undermined the architecture of the ancient world, self-evident notwithstanding exotic peculiarities, fascinating for all the simplicity of the motifs, Wright's work convinced at once. So firm of structure for all their movability were the piled up masses growing as it were out of the soil, so natural was the interlacing of the elements shifting as on a cinematographic screen, so reasonable was the arrangement of the spaces, that nobody doubted the inevitable necessity of this form-language for ourselves too, since it was assumed as a matter of course that practicalness and comfort had here been combined into a beautiful synthesis in the only manner possible in our day, that Wright, the artist,

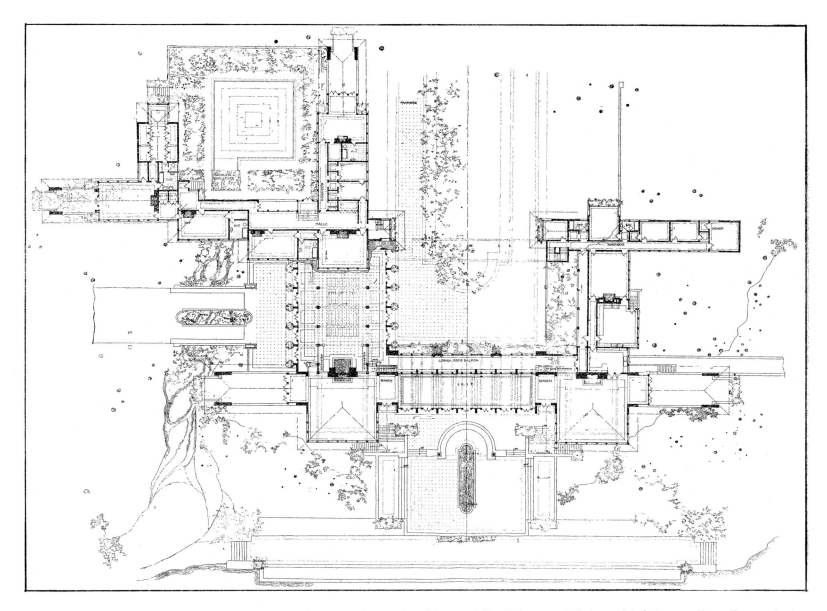

had achieved what Wright, the prophet, had professed, that now the example — the long sought for — had been found, in which universal meaning and individual result were absolutely one, in short, that, in this case personality was universality again. In addition to which — and to this many were certainly not indifferent — the application of Wright's means, even where they were applied less faultlessly, with less virtuosity than by the master, appeared as a rule to warrant a tolerable even a piquant effect!

Thus did the architecture of Holland, Germany, Czecho-Slovakia, France, Belgium, Poland, Roumania etc. in its "avant-garde" and all those who, if things are not going too far, like to consider themselves as belonging to this, willingly undergo the influence of this admirable talent. The shifting of the planes, the projecting penthouse-roofs, the repeatedly interrupted and again continued masses, the predominantly horizontal development, all typical of Wright's art appear at the time when the spirit of Wright's works began to influence our part of the world, as characteristic features of a considerable portion of modern architectural products in Europe.

Meanwhile it is a mistake which is continually made by critics and to which attention cannot too emphatically be drawn, because in this very misconception lies the reason why Wright's influence on European architecture must be considered a less happy one, — it is a mistake to ascribe the arising of these features exclusively to Wright. For at the time when the adoration of Wright's work by his colleagues on this side the Atlantic had reached its culminating point, European architecture itself was in a state of ferment, and cubism was born. Like the influence of Wright, cubism plays an important part in producing the characteristic forms which found expression in the above-meant current of European architecture. This current itself — as may be apparent — is the result of a blending of two influences: a blending which is not only disappointing, because on either side it points once again to a cult of forms instead of an orientation towards the inner nature, but also because it weakened a tendency — the cubistic one — which bids fair to become of the highest importance for the future of architecture. A tendency moreover which must after all be nearer to Wright himself than the cult of externals

with which he was glorified unintentionally through imitation of his work.

If, in determining the factors which stimulated the rise of the aforesaid phenomena in European architecture, we put cubism next to the influence of Wright, it remains notwithstanding an unquestionable fact, that the fascination of Wright's work smoothed to a great extent the way for cubism itself; and the irony of fate has willed — as was suggested above — that the lyric charm of this architectonic piper of Hammeln at the same time impaired the purity of the sound which began to be heard in the architecture of Europe, in consequence of intentions which must be identical with Wright's, though his works often revealed them in a different manner than his aims (as expressed in his writings).

That which Wright desired, viz., an architecture based on the needs and the possibilities of our own time, satisfying its requirements of general economic feasibility, universal social attainableness, in general of social-aesthetic necessity, and resulting in compactness, austerity and exactness of form, in simplicity and regularity; that which he desired, but from which he continually escaped on the wings of his great visionary faculty, was tried in more actual consistency in cubism.

Cubism in architecture — this should be grasped clearly — arose in complete independence of Wright, just like in free art and suggested by it, from within. Besides superficial external resemblance there was undoubtedly inner affinity with Wright's work — it may be worth while to trace this affinity and with a view to it one should also glance at some of Wright's reliefs — whereas in reality the two were wholly different, nay rather opposed to one another.

They seem to agree in the preference for the right angle, in the three-dimensional tendency, in the breaking up of bodies and again combining their parts, in general in the striving to gather into one whole many small parts — previously obtained through analysis — into a whole which in its appearance still betrays the elements of the original dissection; they have also in common: the application of new materials, new methods, new constructions, the conforming to new demands.

What was with Wright, however, plastic exuberance, sensuous abundance, was in the case of cubism — it could not for the present be otherwise — puritanic asceticism, mental abstinence. What with Wright out of the very fulness of life developed into a luxurious growth which could only suit American "high-life", compelled itself in Europe to the humble level of an abstraction which had its origin in other wants and embraced all: men and things.

Whereas Wright proved to be an artist rather than a prophet, cubism *) paved the way for the more actual execution of that which was his theory too. Since the days of the Renaissance in cubism spoke — after a thirty years' incitement — for the first time again the conscience of architecture: painfully scrupulous as inherent to the years of puberty, but likewise equally strong!

In architecture as in free art cubism was a period of transition; a phase of dissolving the old system and

*) Cubism, viz., as it was originally; not what people were pleased to make of it here and there — especially with us (in Holland!).

building up the new order. The idea of construction and the value of proportions were regained and transferred to another plane; the essential importance of the line and the almost oppressive gravity of the form were recognized anew and sounded to the depth; the insight into the importance of the mass and its complement, space, was recovered again and deepened. But above all in cubism — as the logical continuation of former attemps at renovation — was expressed directly and clearly the tension of a greater, a truer vitality than that which was apparent from the architecture of many previous periods whose independent life was until within recent days confined at best to the sweetly-affecting fitness of a talented, highly cultivated taste.

Thus cubism was an introspection and a beginning as well: it imposed tasks relying on the future, where former generations had laid claims parasitizing on the past. In the involuntary romanticism of its vehement craving after complexity, it was the beginning of a new form-synthesis, of a new — an unhistorical! — classicism.

The need of number and measure, of purity and order, of regularity and repetition, of completeness and finish, properties of the organs of modern life, of our technique, our traffic, our hygiene: inherent also in the state of society, the economic conditions, the mass production, find their precursors in cubism.

There is something tragic in the fact that to the development of things which Wright has advocated so long and so energetically, harm has been and is still being done, through misconception of his work, by the dilettantism of his own followers. It may be a matter of indifference to us that with Wright himself the conception of the architect outgrew the consciousness of the preacher: because of the beautiful result, because the basic idea of his work is a reasonable one, not confused by aesthetic premisses, because, lastly, life, which has not become rigid and fixed, continually escapes from the dogma of theory. Theory, however, be this emphasized, is valuable as a basis in life. Valuable always, but altogether indispensable now-a-days, when every aesthetic guidance, each traditional hold is wanting. The new architecture can hardly be too consistent in its aims, and we shall be willing to take into the bargain the inevitable inconsistencies of its results, should they be worthy.

We cannot insist too much with the disciples of Wright — as he used to do himself —, that carrying on the good work Wright began is a different thing from what they call "to be inspired" by his work. It is no less wrong to imitate what a great contemporary has built than to copy a Greek column: on the contrary. More harmful, indeed, than the impediments which an academic architecture puts in the way of a rising functional art of building, are the works of those who imitate modern masters, because the second-hand appearance in which the latter clothe their products, shirks the struggle for pure building, owing to its actual form and its pretence of organic growth, whereas the Academics honestly expose their front to the attack. And if anything is "pernicious" for the future of the new architecture, it is this half-heartedness, which is worse than frankly plagiarism, which is lack of character.

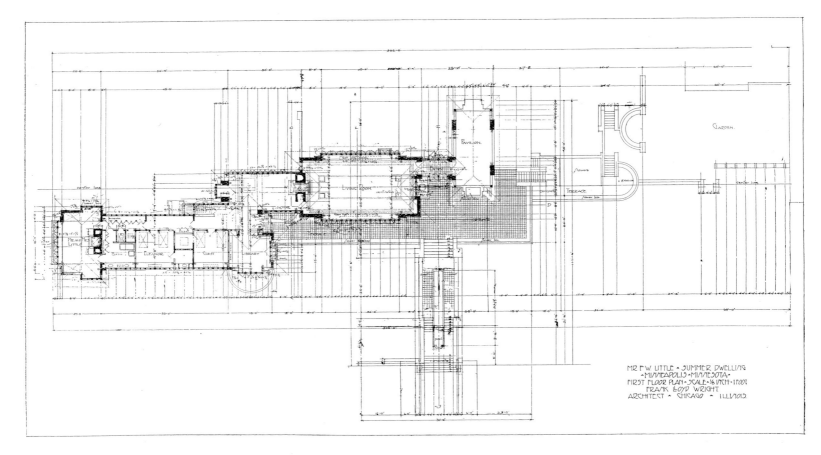

MR F.W. LITTLE • SUMMER DWELLING
• MINNEAPOLIS • MINNESOTA •
FIRST FLOOR PLAN • SCALE ⅛ INCH • 1 FOOT
FRANK LLOYD WRIGHT
ARCHITECT • CHICAGO • ILLINOIS

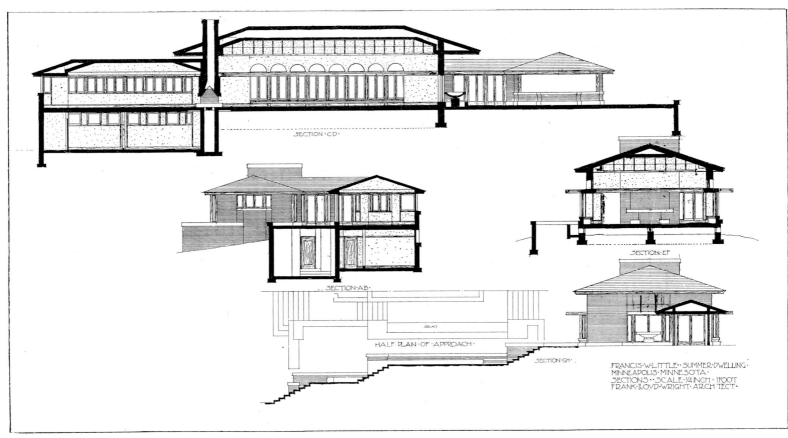

SECTION • CD •

SECTION • EF •

SECTION • AB •

HALF PLAN OF APPROACH •

SECTION • GH •

FRANCIS • W • LITTLE • SUMMER • DWELLING •
MINNEAPOLIS • MINNESOTA •
SECTIONS • • SCALE ¼ INCH • 1 FOOT
FRANK • LLOYD • WRIGHT • ARCHITECT •

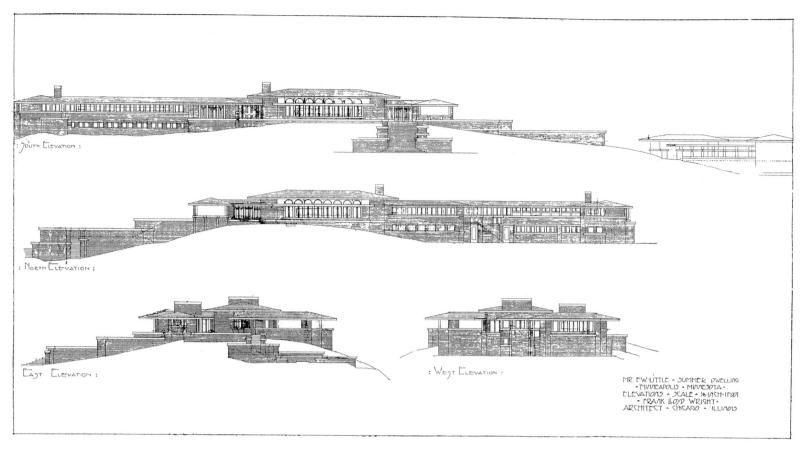

: South Elevation :

: North Elevation :

: East Elevation :

: West Elevation :

MR. F. W. LITTLE · SUMMER DWELLING
· MINNEAPOLIS · MINNESOTA ·
ELEVATIONS · SCALE · 1⁄8 INCH·1·FOOT
· FRANK LLOYD WRIGHT ·
ARCHITECT · CHICAGO · ILLINOIS

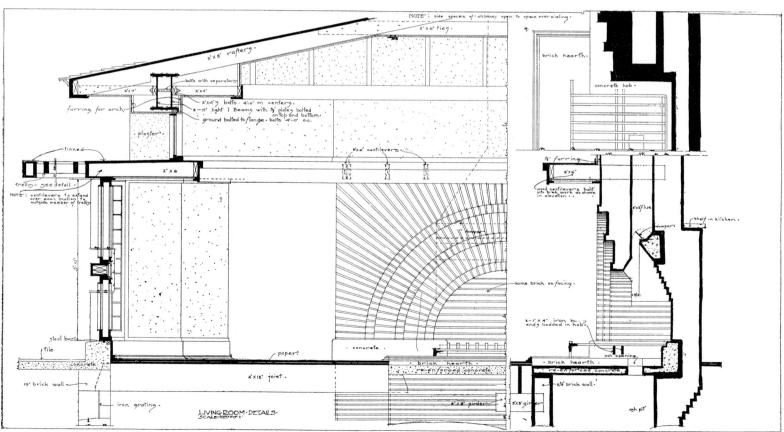

LIVING·ROOM·DETAILS·
SCALE·1⁄2"·FOOT·

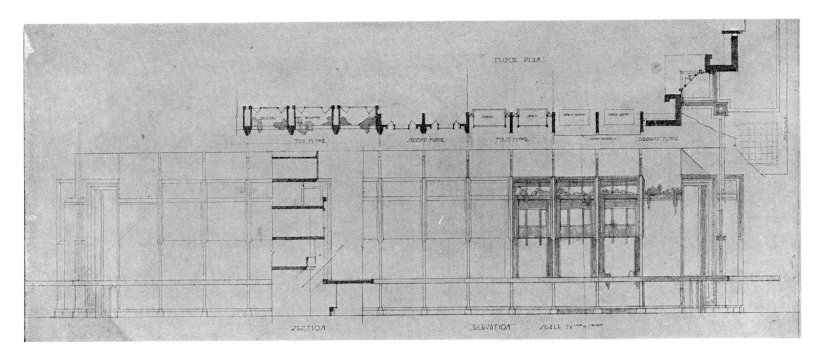

□ FRANK LLOYD WRIGHT □ ET L'ARCHITECTURE NOUVELLE PAR ROB. MALLET-STEVENS □ 1925*

L'architecture moderne n'est pas une mode, elle est un besoin. L'architecture moderne n'est pas décorative, elle est utile et normale. Il y a entre l'architecture rococo de l'époque de Louis XV et l'architecture moderne, la même différence qu'entre un carrosse peinturluré, chargé d'ornements et de rocailles de la „guerre en dentelles" et une voiture automobile toute unie aux éléments profilés. Pendant des siècles on s'est servi de la pierre pour construire. Chaque époque a marqué son empreinte sur la pierre, l'ornement seul définissant un style, sans toutefois le style ogival où le mode de construction a modifié l'esthétique. Si nous reprenons l'exemple du véhicule, il en est de même: un cheval, des brancards, une caisse, des roues; et ces organes indispensables décorés suivant le goût et la mode du moment. Brusquement, tout change: le béton armé apparait bouleversant les procédés de construction, le moteur à explosion remplace le cheval. La science crée une esthétique nouvelle. Les formes sont profondément modifiées, la maison ou la voiture étant intégralement différentes. Les baies étroites et hautes s'expliquaient: la pierre n'autorise pas des linteaux de grande portée, de grandes baies représentent des surfaces de refroidissement dangereuses. Avec le béton armé et le chauffage central, l'architecte peut distribuer l'air et la lumière par des fenêtres d'énormes dimensions, les linteaux peuvent s'allonger en large. L'aspect extérieur de la maison se trouve totalement autre.

Les porte à faux, les poteaux de sections réduites, les points d'appui rares donnent de suite une autre allure au bâtiment.

Les architectes qui ont compris les ressources formidables du béton armé sont rares. S'il est vrai qu'actu-ellement tous les constructeurs font appel au béton armé, les artistes craignent encore l'emploi de formes nouvelles et leur imagination paresseuse préfère les styles passés.

Frank Lloyd Wright fut un des premiers à oser, à rompre avec une tradition très voisine de la routine, pour créer. Et son oeuvre est grande, riche, logique.

L'Amérique sans passé, il faut bien le dire, avait le droit de choisir entre tous les styles celui qui convenait le mieux à ses besoins, à ses goûts et à ses habitudes. En effet, il y a seulement cinquante ans, un palais, un immeuble ou une villa pouvait en Amérique être de style ogival, Louis XVI ou Empire sans inconvénient. S'inspirant des styles „passés" des autres pays plus âgés, rien ne plaidait plus en faveur d'un style que d'un autre. Et j'avoue qu'un gratte-ciel américain traité dans le goût de l'architecture monastique médiévale n'était pas beaucoup plus ridicule qu'une gare de chemin de fer européenne bâtie en style Louis XVI.

Survint le béton armé. Les américains furent assez longtemps réfractaires à ce mode de construction; le fer régnait en maître dans l'art de bâtir. Cependant les ingénieurs américains édifiaient de splendides usines. Certaines constructions industrielles sont d'une grande beauté; on sent un programme net et clair, une conception saine et économique, une logique qui s'impose; il s'en suit une esthétique extrèmement agréable. C'est une architecture vraie et sincère.

Wright, sans s'en inspirer en quoique ce soit, a connu, a vu ces constructions aux lignes originales (non pas de cette originalité qui consiste à exécuter systématiquement le contraire de ce que l'on voit d'habitude, mais cette originalité faite d'un problème à résoudre différent de ceux posés jusqu'alors), Wright a vécu dans cette ambiance de constructions saines. Nous pourrions dire, nous autres européens sevrés de toute recherche depuis un siècle (sans la Tour Eiffel) que sa tâche était plus aisée que la nôtre! Nous, architectes

---

*[See translation, page 163.]

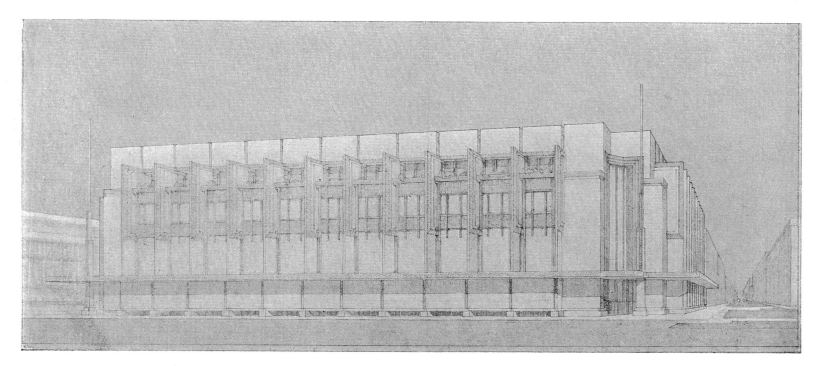

du vieux monde, avions à démolir le fatras décoratif du XIXe siècle dans une atmosphère hostile; avant de songer à créer, il fallait mettre à bas l'ornementation excessive et arbitraire de toute l'époque de plagiat, d'indifférence et de paresse.

Mais quelle plus belle récompense que de voir s'élever sur tous les points du monde des oeuvres d'hommes ayant la même pensée, le même idéal. Car, fait unique dans l'histoire de l'art, malgré l'imprimerie, la photographie, les expositions, les communications rapides, les revues de propagande, les congrès, les sociétés, le cinématographe, tous ces architectes se sont ignorés les uns les autres, ils n'ont rien su de leurs recherches personnelles et tout d'un coup un style est né, spontanément, universel.

Wright inconnu, même des professionnels, hier encore, prendra rang bientôt dans le phalange des grands créateurs. Et son oeuvre aura une énorme influence, comme celle d'ailleurs de ses confrères qui „voient" comme lui. L'architecture de Wright est humaine, elle est vraie et sera comprise et aimée partout. Le régionalisme est mort, la maison de l'homme, à peu de chose près, est la même sur tous les points du globe civilisé, sa beauté doit être la même.

La mode bientôt entrera en jeu. C'est fatal. On sent déjà dès maintenant certaines tendances, je n'ose dire certaines formules, le mot est trop sévère, qui prennent corps. On a cité le mot: architecture horizontale. En soi, la chose est bonne pour des habitations de peu d'étages; les baies étirées en large amènent fatalement des parallèles horizontales, il y aurait à craindre que les architectes sans idée, sans talent, ceux qui ont toujours copié le passé (et quelle copie!) ne se hâtent en présence de la faveur de ces lignes nouvelles, de copier comme toujours, sans esprit et sans logique. Ces artistes sans conscience s'emparent d'une idée qui est belle, la déforment et la ridiculisent au point d'amener la masse à aspirer vers autre chose. Des

oeuvres de la force de celles de Wright sont impossibles à plagier, mais on sent déjà avec terreur, les efforts faits par ces architectes opportunistes pour s'en emparer et exploiter ce vol.

Tous mes confrères savent le respect et l'admiration très sincères que j'ai pour l'oeuvre de Wright, et cela depuis des années, je puis donc me permettre certaines petites critiques.

Nous avons là, sous les yeux quelques compositions du maitre, d'une valeur architectonique incontestable, mais certains toits me paraissent inutiles. On nous a souvent reproché de supprimer systématiquement les toitures „ces chapeaux des maisons". D'abord, une maison ne s'habille pas et peut être très belle sans chapeau, témoins les admirables constructions couvertes en terrasses de l'Italie et du XVIIIe siècle français. Ensuite le toit onéreux (charpente, couverture) n'est pas accessible, et sans vouloir vivre sur sa maison, il est bien agréable de pouvoir profiter de cet espace libre dominant alentour. D'autre part, la construction en béton armé, (à l'heure actuelle) n'appelle pas de toiture. Pour franchir l'espace à couvrir, la charpente est inutile. Et combien est plus belle la ligne nette qui finit la maison.

Ceci dit, les compositions de Wright comme plans et comme élévations sont comparables aux grands classiques. Wright fait jouer ses volumes dans l'espace avec maîtrise, sans tomber dans la recherche piteuse du pittoresque, ses compositions ont une fantaisie ordonnée, un rythme attrayant qui dégagent une impression de gaieté et de bien-être.

Formulons un voeu: sans le copier, que ses confrères américains s'imprègnent de son oeuvre, l'aiment comme nous l'aimons. Si certains architectes des Etats Unis ont conçus de belles constructions, Wright est avec eux et il est à la meilleure place.

□   □   □   □

DWELLING ... AT ... PASADENA ... CALIFORNIA ... FOR
MRS ... GEORGE ... MADISON ... MILLARD
F L L WRIGHT ... ARCHITECT ... LOS ANGELES

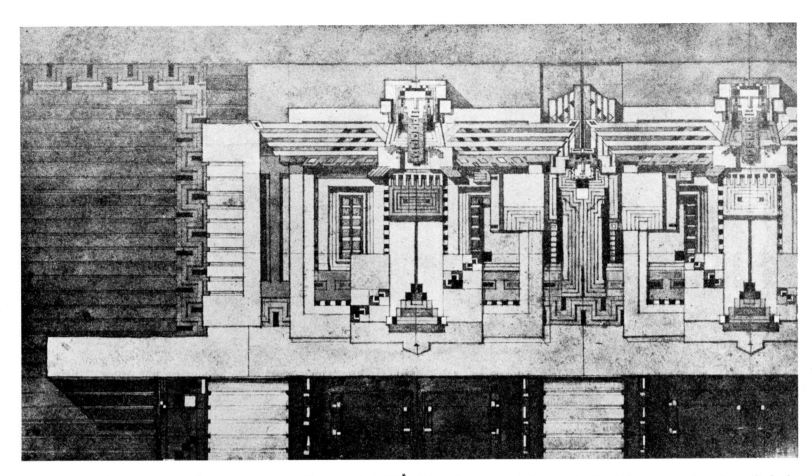

FRANK LLOYD WRIGHT*
▢ ▢ VON ERICH MENDELSOHN ▢ ▢

DAS NACHTSTEHENDE ENTSPRINGT EINER DISKUSSION MIT MR. FISKE KIMBAL∣L – PHILADELPHIA, DER IN WASMUTH-MONATSHEFTEN HEFT 6/1925 ÜBER DEN „SIEG DES JUNGEN KLASSIZISMUS ÜBER DEN FUNKTIONALISMUS DER 90ER JAHRE" SCHRIEB. ▢ ▢ ▢ ▢ ▢ ▢ ▢ ▢ ▢ ▢ ▢

Frank Lloyd Wright's Werk ist umkämpft.
Die auf die Immergültigkeit der historischen Formen eingeschworene Partei lehnt sein Werk ab.
Die den Angstblick auf die Historie ablehnende Partei schwört auf sein Werk.
Ueber Frank Lloyd Wright schreiben, heisst deshalb, sich mit beiden Parteien auseinandersetzen.
Sein Werk als notwendig betrachten, heisst sich objektiv beiden Lagern gegenüber verhalten.
Frank Lloyd Wright lieben, heisst, sich für das eine Lager entschieden haben: für das frische Wagnis, unsere eigene Zeit zu gestalten.
Gelingt der Versuch, diese Voraussetzung in Beweis und Gegenbeweis logisch durchzuführen, so fällt der Vorwurf der Voreingenommenheit, der Selbstverteidigung oder der Selbstliebe.
Unwissende oder Schulmeister, die beide vor der Wahrheit unsicher werden, haben also nichts zu befürchten.
Denn alsdann werden Wortgefechte keine Entscheidung herbeiführen, Luftspiegelungen keine Klarheit bringen.
Vielmehr ist an einen Weg zu denken, der beiden Parteien ein gemeinsames Ziel verspricht. ▢

Die Gegenpartei nennt Sullivan und seine Schule einen Impressionisten.
Sie meint das im Sinne der impressionistischen Malerei der Mitte des vergangenen Jahrhunderts. Diese bildet, auf dem Tiefstand ihrer Entwicklung, die Natur nach, indem sie, ganz gleich durch welche malerischen Mittel, den momentanen Eindruck auf den Vermittler wiedergibt und von dem Grad der erreichten Naturtreue den Schönheitswert des Bildes abhängig macht.
Dieser Vorwurf trifft den Sullivan der Weltausstellung Chicago 1893. Denn sein „Verkehrsgebäude" ist nur äusserlich neu, im Ornament und im Detail.
Während nämlich die naturalistische Nachahmung in der impressionistischen Malerei das entscheidende Moment ist für die Struktur des ganzen Bildes, bleibt sie, als Ornament oder Bauform, in der Architektur nur eine Zutat der zweiten Dimension und hat nichts zu tun mit dem eigentlichen architektonischen Element, der Dreidimensionalität des Raumes.
Deshalb besteht zwischen Attwoods „Kunstpalast" derselben Ausstellung und Sullivan's „Verkehrsgebäude", trotz der grundverschiedenen Zweckbestimmung, kein Unterschied im struktiven Aufbau, sondern nur in der Anwendung des ornamentalen Idioms.
Gedanke und Handlung sind die gleichen, beides sind rein repräsentative Dekorationen, nur Wort und Geste sind verschieden.
Säule bleibt Säule, ganz gleich, ob sie mit gräzisierendem oder romanisierendem Blattwerk geschmückt ist, ob sie als Säule den Architrav trägt, oder als Pfeiler den Rundbogen. Theater bleibt Theater, auch wenn es sich als lebendiges Sein aufführt.

---

*[See translation, page 164.]

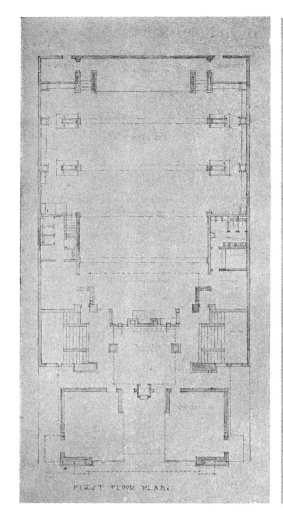
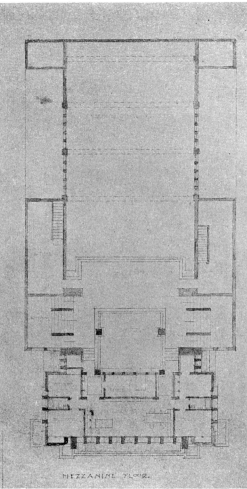
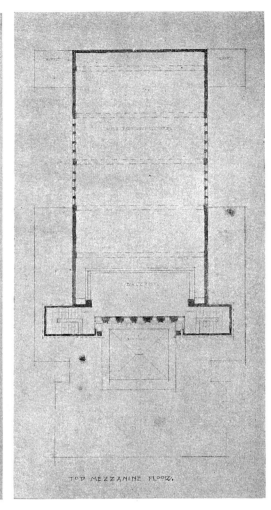

FIRST FLOOR PLAN.   MEZZANINE FLOOR.   TOP MEZZANINE FLOOR.

Nur in diesem Sinn also hat die Unterscheidung: Sullivan sei naturalistisch, Attwood abstrakt schön: Berechtigung. Aber sie berührt nicht das Wesen der Architektur.

Weit eher ist Sullivan's „Verkehrsgebäude" als eine erste Stufe seiner Entwicklung, vielleicht jeder neuen Einsicht, aufzufassen.

Denn den Schwächling verführt die Unzufriedenheit mit der alltäglichen, brüchig gewordenen Form zur Flucht, den Mutigen aber treibt sie zum Experiment. Unzufriedenheit allein hat aber nie die Kraft, neue Fundamente zu schaffen. Sie führt höchstens, wie spaeter in Wien, zu einer Secession.

Also war der Weg des Impressionismus falsch. Aber er hätte seiner Natur nach nicht unbedingt falsch zu sein brauchen.

Denn bei vertiefter Einstellung hätte gerade die Erkenntnis der Naturvorgänge anstatt zur Naturnachahmung zur Abstrahierung führen müssen, das heisst, die Kenntnis der organischen und funktionsgemässen Naturgesetze zur Erkenntnis der Elemente im Kunstwerk — in der Malerei: der Farbharmonie und Proportion, in der Architektur: der Konstruktion und des Aufbaues. Gegen diesen falschen Weg der Naturnachahmung oder der rein formalen, der „secessionistischen" Neuerung wendet sich die zweite Stufe in Sullivan's Leben.

Hier nennt die Gegenpartei S u l l i v a n gleichzeitig einen Realisten, indem sie seinen Realismus, ebenfalls noch auf der Basis des Impressionismus, als Imitation des Naturvorbildes auslegen will.

Aber die Theorie, dass auch die Architektur, dieses durch das Hirn des Menschen erzeugte — gedachte und geschaute — Produkt, von den Erscheinungsformen der organischen Natur auf ihr eigenes Wesen schliessen dürfe, verführt dazu, ganz äusserlich und spieltriebmässig den konstruktiven Bedingungen der Organismen nur Linien, also nur Formen zu entlehnen.

Und während Europa sich blindlings auf diesen Irrweg stürzt, aus Ueberdruss am überkommenen Formalismus und nicht aus Mangel an neuen Bauaufgaben, im Jugendstil aufrauscht und sich im Linienspiel schnell zerreibt, bewundert viele Jahre schon zuvor Sullivan das Organisationsvorbild der Natur. Bewundert ihre Folgerichtigkeit, die Ordination und Subordination aller "Organismen", das Ineinandergreifen der einzelnen Teile, also das Absolute ihrer Gesetzmässigkeit, nicht die zufälligen Erscheinungen ihrer "Organe".

Und so widerlegt Sullivan's "Guaranty Gebäude" Buffalo 1896 die Gegenpartei, wenn sie ihre impressionistische "organische Theorie" verallgemeinert und auf sein Werk bezieht. Das "Guaranty-Gebäude" ist, wie Kimball selbst zugibt, "einfach, kristallinisch, aus einem Guss", das heisst, es ist absolut, organisch und also frei von jeder Zufälligkeit. Im Gefühl freilich ist es noch übersteigert. Der neugefundene Baustoff, das Eisen, dessen wirkliche Beanspruchungsmöglichkeiten damals noch nicht zu Ende gedacht sind, übersteigert seine Phantasie.

Die grössere Leistungsfähigkeit des Materials erlaubt ein bisher unbekanntes Anwachsen der Dimension.
Beide, Material und Dimension, verleiten ihn zum Dithyrambus der Vertikalen.
Aber Eisenkonstruktion und Vertikalismus sind durchaus keine Bedingung auf Gegenseitigkeit. Das Konstruktions-Schema des Wolkenkratzers ist bis auf die heutige Zeit das Fachwerk. Dieses bleibt Fachwerk, also ein Gitter, ob es in Holz wie ehedem, oder wie heute in Eisen gebaut wird. Das bedeutet die fast völlige Gleichwertigkeit der Vertikalen und der Horizontalen.
Aber diese Uebersteigerung der Vertikalen erscheint ebenso wie die Binderahnungen in den besten Werken Olbrich's und van de Velde's hier als Gesicht der kommenden funktionsgemässen Möglichkeiten. Sie ist also mehr Vorausfühlung als tatsächliche Neugeburt.
Was bei Sullivan noch als Reaktion der Vernunft gegen die Unvernunft der formalen Dekoration auftritt, ist keine "funktionelle Mode", sondern logisches Ergebnis der gesamten Lebenserscheinungen.
Denn einst war — im Entstehen — auch das griechische Schema funktionell, das heisst in diesem Sinn durchaus realistisch.
Diese Tatsache negieren, heisst die Entstehungsgeschichte der geschlossenen Kulturen — der Stile — überhaupt leugnen. Leugnen, das Aegyptens Säulenmassen der Wüste und dem Granit, dass die Säulenhallen Griechenlands dem Mittelmeerduft und dem

Marmor, dass die Pfeilersynkopen des Nordens dem Wetterwechsel und dem Backstein mit ihren Ursprung verdanken.
So steht also der Sullivan der zweiten Stufe, wie jeder Mensch des Uebergangs, zwischen den Dingen.
In der Uebersteigerung seines Realismus kann er den Vorwurf der Gegenpartei, den sie aus ihrer impressionistischen Einstellung heraus erhebt, nicht völlig entkräften.
Aber nur in dieser romantischen Uebersteigerung.
Im Wesentlichen hat sein Realismus den Schritt zum Konstruktivismus schon getan, das heisst begonnen, die konstruktiven, die Wachstumsbedingungen der Organismen sinngemäss in die konstruktiven Elemente der Architektur zu übertragen und anstatt eines sichtbaren Linienspiels das Skelett des Baues fühlbar gemacht.
Damit vollzieht sich in Sullivan der historische Sprung von der impressionistischen Destruktion zur Neustabilisierung des konstruktiven Gesetzes.
Also ist Sullivan der "letzte grosse Führer des Alten", aber zugleich Vorläufer des Neuen.
Dieses Neue schon jetzt sicher zu fixieren, zumindest den genauen Punkt seiner kritischen Kurve anzugeben, ist unmöglich.
Wir kennen noch nicht die letzte Schnelligkeit.
Aber das revolutionäre Spiel der Zug- und Druckkräfte in Eisen und Eisenbeton, die jeder kühnen Konstruktion folgende Geschmeidigkeit der Hilfsbaustoffe haben dem Bau die bisherige Gebundenheit und Schwere ge-

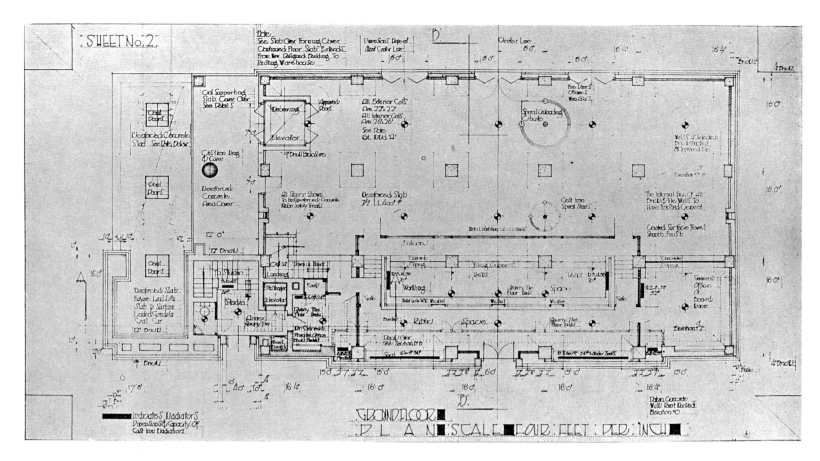

nommen. Jedenfalls beweist die Leidenschaftlichkeit, mit der sich die beiden Parteien bekämpfen, dass es bei diesem Kampf um mehr geht als um eine Mode. Beide kämpfen um die Elemente, ohne die sie nicht leben können.

Das Elementare ist aber das Gemeinsame.

Hier wird das Ziel sichtbar, nur der Standpunkt ist verschieden.

Augen rückwärts, Geist gebunden und verzagt.

Augen vorwärts, Geist frei und hoffend.

Die Klassizisten suchen die Form als das Primäre. Das bedeutet auf dem Wege zum Element einen Umweg. Denn das Suchen der Formelemente ist gewissermassen eine Aufgabe der intellektuellen Rechnung, als Schlussergebnis einer Reihe von Formeln, das richtig sein wird, wenn die Voraussetzungen stimmen.

Ein bequemer Weg, unkühn und hinter der Zeit herlaufend. Wir aber, suchen die Elemente an sich, die Form erst als logisches Ergebnis.

Das ist der Weg der Intuition, des kühnen Gesichtes, des freien Denkens oder, wenn man will, des Experimentes. Als solcher nicht ohne Gefahr. Denn er ist schwer kontrollierbar und oft verbaut durch das Nachhinken der technischen Möglichkeiten. Oft auch irrend in den Mitteln, weil er nur das Ziel sieht, ohne den Weg zu errechnen.

Beide Wege sind ohne Tradition nicht denkbar.

Tradition reisst nie ab. Jedes Werk ist zeitgeboren, zeitbedingt.

Zeit folgt auf Zeit.

Aber es gibt Hindernisse, welche die gewohnte Entwicklungsfolge stören.

Dann ist es richtig, einen neuen Weg zu suchen.

So gesehen, haben beide Wege ihre Berechtigung.

Aber der erste kann sich auf die Dauer nicht der hinreissenden Kraft des neuen entziehen, der trotz unsäglicher Mühen, öfteren Niederlagen in immer wieder jugendlichem Aufstieg sein Ziel erreicht.

Der zweite kann nicht ständig im Versuch leben, sondern muss letzen Endes sich bereitfinden zur Ruhe der Befriedigung, um das Gefundene auszuwerten und zu geniessen.

Der erste also wird gezwungen, sich seiner historischen Form zu entkleiden — zur Nacktheit des Neuen, der zweite wird nackt geboren.

Dann erkennen beide sich als gleicher Art. Unter dem Zwang unseres Lebens, unserer Zeit wird zeitgeboren, aus Material und Konstruktion, die Form, der Stil. □

Allein von solchem Standort kann F r a n k L l o y d W r i g h t betrachtet werden.

Sein Werk steht mitten in unserer Zeit.

Somit ist seine Negierung des Ueberlieferten durchaus positiv.

Seine Entwicklung aus diesem Gedanken vollzieht sich logisch nach organischem Gesetz, wenn auch naturgemäss noch ohne inneren Zwang, den neuen konstruktiven Baustoff im Sinne des Monumentalen restlos durchzubilden.

Vorbildlich die Organisation seiner Bauten, sachlich, frei, geöffnet, bewegt.

Unerschöpflich der Reichtum seiner formbildenden Ideen, bezaubernd die Harmonie seiner Farben.

Ein grosser Künstler, den wir verehren.

Ein grosser Mensch, den wir lieben. □

CONCERNING THE IMPERIAL □ □ HOTEL TOKYO, JAPAN □ □ BY LOUIS H. SULLIVAN □ 1923

On the vast stage of the world drama, two ideas both of them immense in power, confront each other in spectacular appeal to the fears and the courage of mankind. And it is precisely this condition that gives animus and validity to what is to follow in contemplation of the Imperial Hotel, of Tokyo, Japan, as a high act of courage — an utterance of man's free spirit, a personal message to every soul that falters, and to every heart that hopes.

It is becoming clear that a new thought is arising in the world which is destined to displace the old thought. The new thought partakes of the nature of that freedom of which men long have dreamed. It is now breaking through the crust of the old thought which thus far in history has dominated the world of men and which embodies the idea of dominion and of submissive acquiescence.

The old idea, or fetish, is dying because it no longer satisfies the expansion of thought and feeling of which the impressive revelation of modern science are a primary factor; and especially because it is no longer at one with those instincts we call human; it does not recognize the heart as a motive power.

Yet is the old idea tenaciously fixed in the minds of a majority of those engaged in commerce, the industries, the law, the courts of justice, and especially among parasites of all kinds and degrees.

The old idea reaches from top to bottom of the social strata, and also from bottom to top. It is an age-old fixed idea, based upon a concept of self preservation, which once may have had an outward semblance of validity even though its stability of superstructure rested upon a foundation of human slavery, ignorance and suppression.

While in modern times bodily slavery as such has been done away with in theory, the old idea has persisted, curiously transformed into a slavery of the mind, which also ranges through all the social strata, even as men appear to be bodily free.

This new slavery of mind is manifest in a strange, ever-present disturbing fear, anxiety, and incertitude, which permeates society and which leads the individual to cling for safety to the old ideas, superstitions, and taboos, in order that he may conform and not appear too obvious as an individual, a target; that he may, above all, escape the fashionable epithets, "crank", "visionary", "dreamer", "freak". Hence comes about a new economic slavery causing the man, high or low, to fear for his job, and live in a nightmare so terrifying that he dare not say one word that might be construed as disturbing. Such minds in their nature are asleep to the significance of great world movements in thought.

But the idea of freedom is also old; older indeed than the slave-idea. For it is of the nature of any organism that it wishes to be free to grow and expand. This instinctive desire for freedom has been held in check and dominated by the intellectual idea of fear, resulting in unnumbered inhibitions and suppressions, which have led to an obscuration of the minds of men of the two ideas of slavery and freedom.

But the idea of freedom a l s o is beginning to permeate

the thoughts of men, with a new urge, also through all the strata of society, and is massively defining, taking form, and becoming energized, through an ever-growing knowledge and ever-increasing understanding of the true nature, the true status of man not as creature but creator; an enlarging view of man's inherent powers and a growing consciousness that his slavery has been self-imposed. It was in this sense that I have had occasion recently to comment upon the splendid interpretation of the spirit of the Amerian people manifest in the design submitted in the competition for the Tribune Building in Chicago — by a Finlander — Eliel Saarinen.

It is in this sense that we are now about to contemplate the new Imperial Hotel in Tokyo, Japan.

This great work is the masterpiece of Frank Lloyd Wright, a great free spirit, whose fame as a master of ideas is an accomplished world-wide fact.

Through prior visits he had discerned, and added to the wealth of his own rich nature, the spirit, as evidenced in forms of the ideals of Old Japan, which still persist, in slumber, among its living people, needing but the awakening touch.

It is a high faculty of what we call genius to penetrate and temporarily to reside within the genius of another people foreign to our own local ways. And it is this quality of vision, this receptivity, this openness of mind, that especially signalizes the free spirit — the mind free from provincialism and the fear of life.

Next in order to the power of vision comes the power to interpret in thought; and, next to this, the power to express the thought, the state of feeling, in concrete terms.

In this structure is not to be found a single form distinctly Japanese; nor that of any other country; yet in its own individual form, its mass, and subsidiaries, its evolution of plan and development of thesis; in its

sedulous care for niceties of administration, and for the human sense of joy, it has expressed, in inspiring form as an epic poem, addressed to the Japanese people, their inmost thought. It is characterized by the quality, Shibui, a Japanese word, signifying the reward of earnest comtemplation. In studying the concrete expression, the embodiment of idea in solid form, the magnitude of this structure should always be borne in mind. It is 300 X 500 feet on the ground, the area thus equaling 150.000 square feet, or nearly two and one-half times the area covered by the great Auditorium Building in Chicago. The structure is three stories high in the main, with special masses equivalent in height to seven stories.

In a sense it is a huge association of structures, a gathering of the clans, so to speak; it is a seeming aggregate of buildings shielding beauteous gardens, sequestered among them. Yet there hovers over all,

and as an atmosphere everywhere, a sense of primal power in singleness of purpose; a convincing quiet that bespeaks a master hand, guiding and governing.

Upon further analysis, aided by reference to the floor plans, it is disclosed that the structure is not a group, but a single mass; spontaneously subdividing into subsidiary forms in groups or single, as the main function itself flows into varied phases, each seeking expression in appropriate correlated forms, each and all bearing evidence of one controlling mind, of one hand moulding materials like a master craftsman.

It is this coming to grips with realities that infiltrates the mind of the observer, until he feels the reward of earnest contemplation in the sense that what at first he had regarded as a material structure is sending forth to him an emanation of beauty, the presence of a living thing, a wondrous contribution to the architecture of the world, an exposition of the virile thought of modern man.

103

So much for the ever-growing fascination of external forms, which appear as eloquent expressions of a something that must reside within them and justify them, upon logical grounds, as forms developed from functions of utility.

In considerations both of analysis and synthesis one must regard the plan as the mainspring of the work; and this plan in turn as but the organization of the primal purposes of utility, manifold in their nature, of service to be rendered.

Now, in examining the plans at the various floor levels, one discovers that the big idea of service divides into two specialized forms: the first constituting as a complex group a hotel complete in all details for the comfort and entertainment of the traveling public, or residentials; the second, more formal and sumptuous part, is discernible as a group embodiment of the necessity for a clearing-house not only for the social obligations incurred by Japanese official life in its contacts with representatives of other lands, but also for the great social functions now inevitable in the high life of the Capital.

Consequent upon the relation of these two groups there exists a most felicitous system of interpenetrations, and communications, with a circulatory system, all worked out in a manner signifying not only mental grasp but creative imagination, based on the human being as a unit and a motive.

The dispositions throughout the entire building are so dexterously interwoven that the structure as a whole becomes a humanized fabric, in any part of which one feels the all-pervading sense of continuity, and of intimate relationships near and far. In this especial sense the structure. carrying the thought, is unique among hotel buildings throughout the world. Japan is to be felicitated that its superior judgment in the selection of an architect of masterly qualifications, of such nature as to welcome new problems of time and place, has been justified. The longer the contemplation of this work is continued, the more intense becomes the conviction that this Master of Ideas has not only performed a service of distinction, but, far and above this, has presented to the people of Japan, as a free-will offering, a great gift which shall endure for all generations to come

as a world exemplar, most beautiful and inspiring, of which Japan may well be proud among the nations as treasuring it in sole possession.

In further study of the plans in their aspect of economics, one should carefully note the differences of levels, shown thereon but more clearly set forth in the longitudinal section. These differences of level are, in one aspect, a part of the charm of the work considered from the human point of view, and, technically, as a skillful method of deployment. They favor also the interpenetrations and the easy accessibility of the larger units and, thus, the compactness of arrangement and economy of space. A notable feature in this regard is the location of a single great kitchen, centrally placed in such wise as to serve the cabaret directly, the main restaurant directly, the private dining rooms by stair-

ways and capacious electric service elevators, and likewise the banquet hall and ballroom above.

Beneath the banquet hall is a theatre seating 1.000, and at the level of the main floor of the theatre the entire structure is traversed and in a manner bisected by a grand promenade twenty feet in width and 300 feet in length. This promenade brings the two long wings of guest rooms in touch with the central group and acts as a foyer from which are entered the theatre, four groups of private dining rooms, and opposite the theatre a large parlor, the projecting balcony of which overlooks the restaurant. The floor of the promenade is sixteen feet above sidewalk level. Beneath the promenade at the north end is situated the formal social entrance with attendant service rooms and hallway leading to passenger elevators. Spaciously around the intersection point of the axis of the promenade with the central axis of the grand-plan are grouped stairways, passenger elevators, service elevators, service stairs, and other utilities. Within this group the service element nt is logically vertical. Elsewhere the circulation is mainly in the horizontal sense, as there are but three tiers of guest rooms.

The two great wings, each 500 feet in length, contain the guest rooms, 285 in number, to be hereinafter described. These two huge parallel masses act as guardians of the inner courts, the gardens, and the more open structural effects, protecting them against the heavy prevailing winds and insuring a large measure of quiet, a sense of retirement and relief from a busy and noisy world without.

There remains to be considered an introductory group, placed within the open space bounded by the main guest wings and the formal social group, and lying symmetrically along the main axis of the grand-plan. It is connected to the wings by means of open bridges over terraces, leading to elevators and stairways. This group constitutes the welcoming feature of a grandiose and most hospitable plan — a plan based upon a rare sense of human nature, everywhere discernible throughout the structure.

At the western, or initial, beginning of the grand-plan, the parallel wings throw out minor wings of an enfolding character. Between these two wings lies a large formal pool, on each side of which are the driveways for automobiles. For jinrikishas separate entrances and runs are provided through the main wings. The entrance feature of the central group stands well back from the pool. One ascends a few steps and enters a spacious vestibule, from which lead up and down special stairways. A broad flight carries one to the main lobby from which one may enter the lounges, the side wings, or directly ahead, the main restaurant. At higher levels the group contains tea rooms, library, roof garden; and

below, the executive offices, the bazaar, and the swimming pool. Beautiful form combinations and vistas make the interior treatment highly interesting and inviting. The level of the restaurant floor is seven feet above the sidewalk grade and nine feet below the grand promenade. The latter is reached from it by means of stairways, upper-level terraces or by elevators.

It cannot too often be reiterated that the terrace idea is the key to the development of the plan in its entirety and that this idea, seized upon by the constructive creative imagination, and carried into logical and beautiful extension, reveals the secret of the serenity and joy of this edifice. Nowhere is the sense of size oppressive, for the eye finds interest everywhere. Thus the structure may truly be called epic, as one views its large simplicity of utterance and richness of well ordered detail. Peculiarly entrancing in this latter regard is the treatment of the lava within and without the structure. Everywhere its surface is wrought in intricate pattern. Constantly varying in expression in accord with location, and so beautifully conceived and cut as to appear of it, integral with it, not applied. The effect is of a continuous, velvety shimmer of lava surface.

Among functional details are to be noted the system of external night-lighting, organically incorporated in large perforated units within the masonry at carefully considered strategic points; the terraced bridges which seem to float; the sumptuous treatment of the entrance to the social group; the recognition of the terminals of elevator shafts and of dumbwaiters. These latter utilitarian things are not hidden or denied, they are affirmed, as they should be, and add to the fullness and fidelity of expression. Indeed, it seems to be but little understood that fidelity to the finer truths inhering in material things is of the essence of romance. And this is a romantic edifice, heroic, dramatic and lyric in expression of function and of form.

A notable selection of local materials has been adopted for the external effects: hand-made brick and hewn lava are chiefly used with a most interesting interspersion of copper for the cornices and delicately worked copper roofs. All flat roofs are of concrete and are treated as gardens.

The color effect is quiet, yet piquant. The bricks are buff, the lava greenish yellow with deep brown spots, the copper turquoise. Minor color effects are secured in various materials, while to all of these effects appertains the added charm of gardens, and distributed shrubs and flowers — all of which are daily cared for; and potted and vased effects are renewed as occasion requires and the changing seasons suggest.

The general construction of the building is definitely based upon the reinforced-concrete-slab idea, carried out by the architect theoretically and practically to its

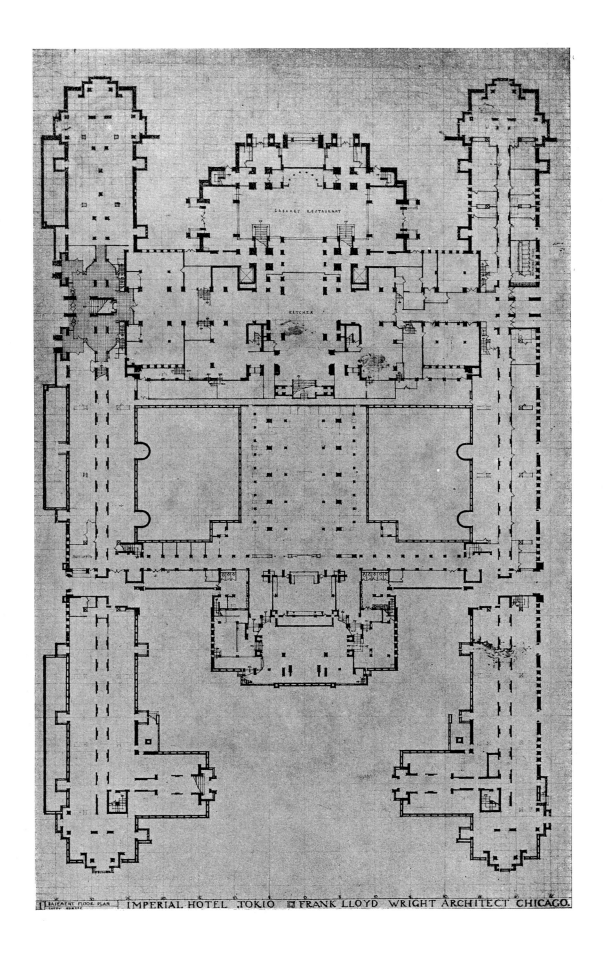

BASEMENT FLOOR PLAN   IMPERIAL HOTEL TOKIO   FRANK LLOYD WRIGHT ARCHITECT CHICAGO.

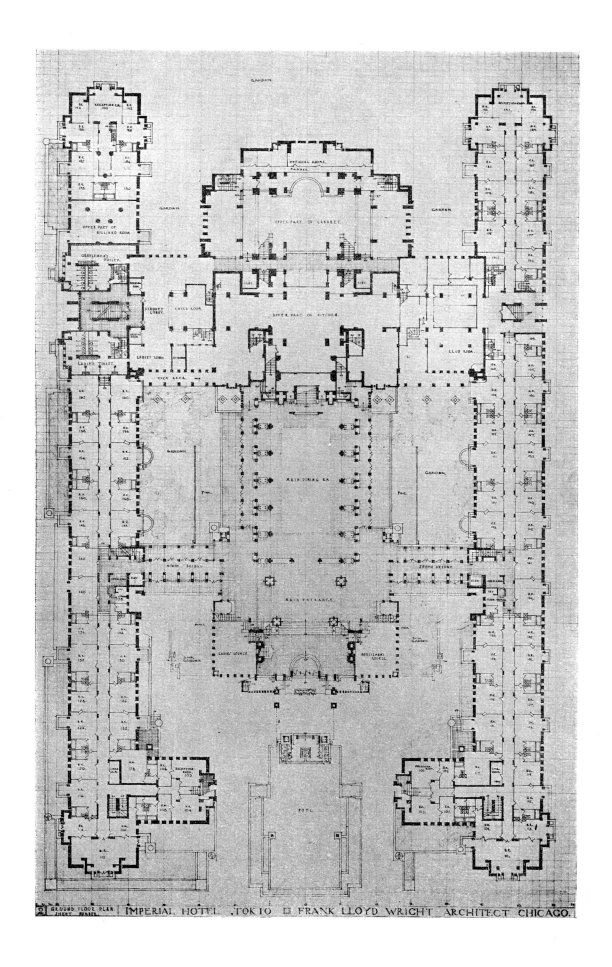

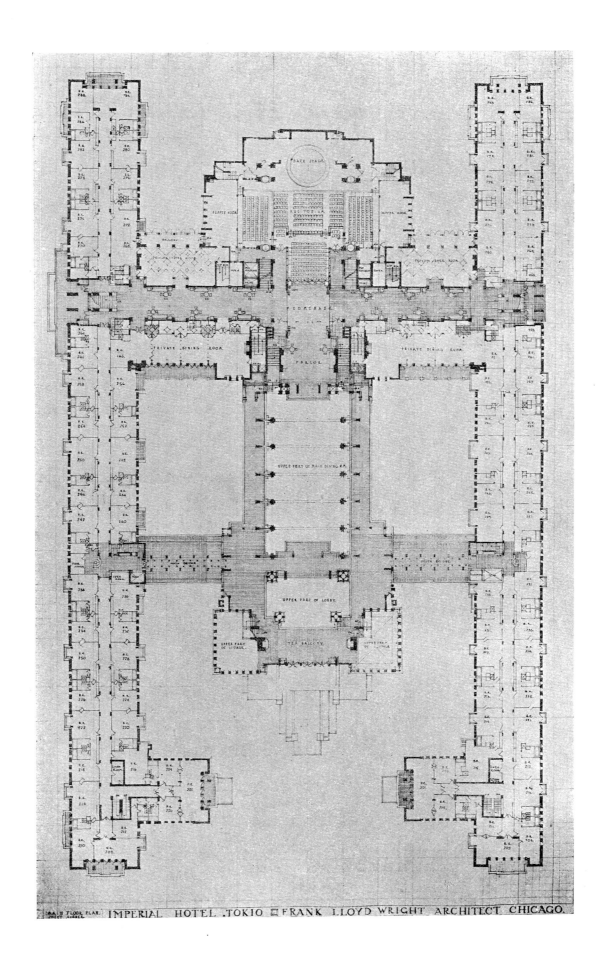

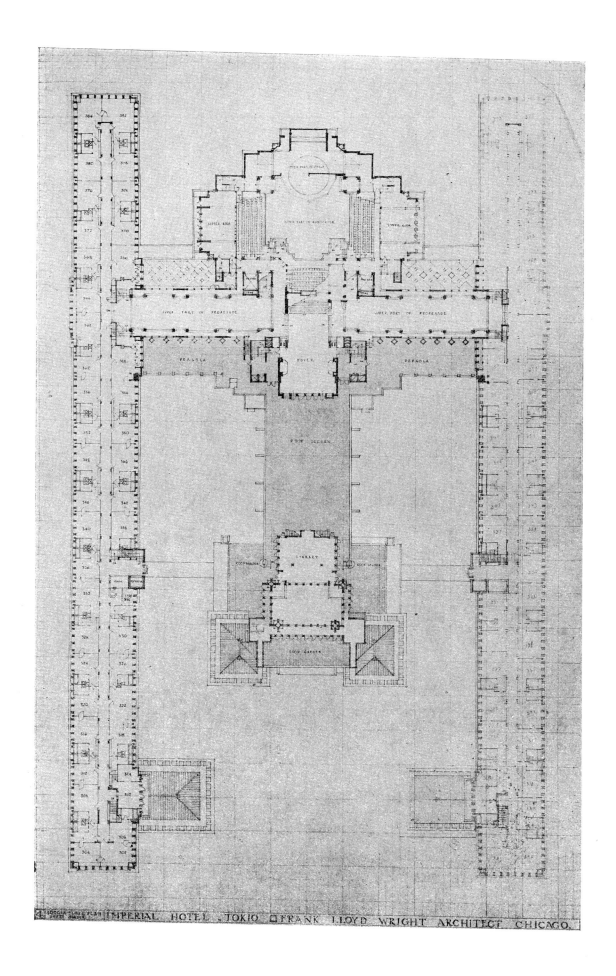

IMPERIAL HOTEL · TOKIO ☐ FRANK LLOYD WRIGHT ARCHITECT CHICAGO.

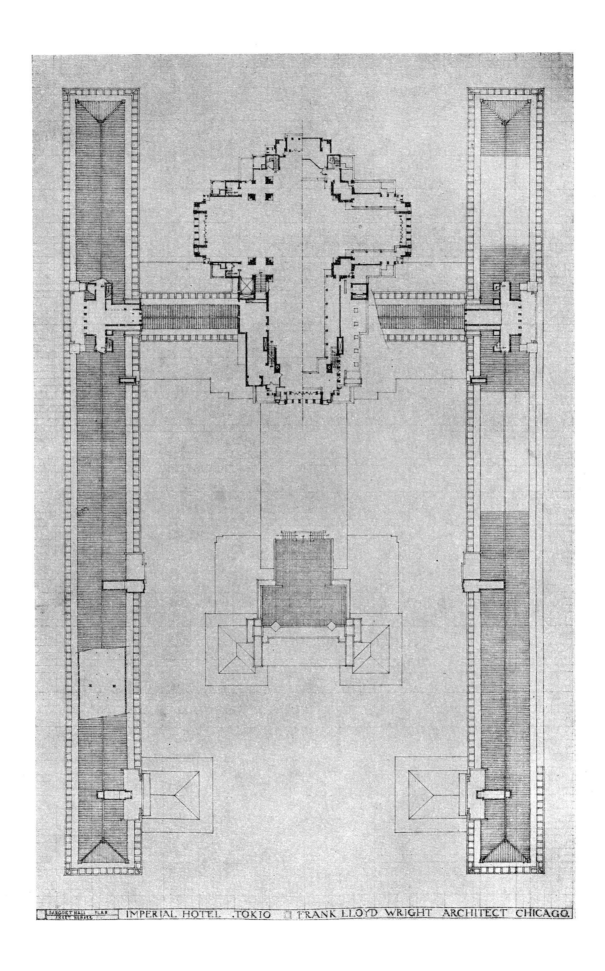

limits, in a manner so novel, so logical, so convincing, as to be of the highest technical interest to those familiar with the general slab idea. The specific application here has to do directly with a flexible resistance to earth-quakes — developing shocks, undulations, oscillations, and twists, in action.

The entire structure rests upon a layer of spongy soil, beneath which is found mud of undetermined depth. Short concrete piles are inserted in the upper layer, where required and as numerous as required, capped by reinforced concrete slabs which receive their direct loads at calculated points. The entire structure thus rests upon a flexible foundation which is free to yield to the mutations of earthquake disturbance and come back to place again.

By a system of distribution of steel rods everywhere the masonry superstructure is knitted thoroughly together in such wise as to render it yielding but resilient, hence secure against fracture or distortion. The slabs are as tenaciously yet flexibly adjusted to the vertical supports, and, where occasion requires, the slab system merges from the concept of lintel into that of cantilever. There is here so general a use of this latter method, on account of its adaptability to projecting horizontal slabs otherwise unsupported and the resulting ease of creating unobstructed areas, that it may perhaps be described as in essence a reinforced-cantilever-slab-system.

In the construction of all outer walls wooden forms were dispensed with; the outer layer of specially notched bricks, and the inside layer of hollow bricks, serving as such. In the cavity between, rods, vertical and horizontal, were placed, and then the concrete filler, the wall thus becoming a solid mass of varied materials,

into which the floor slabs are so solidly tied as to take on the character of cantilevers, as conditions of disturbance might demand.

Thus we have a structure almost literally h a n d m a d e — the use of machinery having proved relatively inefficient — a structure so solidly built of materials inseparably united as to possess all the virtues of a monolith, and yet so completely threaded through with steel fibres as to add the virtues of elasticity and resilience.

The policy of administration of actual construction work was based upon the traditional habits of the Japanese skilled laborer and craftsman. These active and tireless little men are so deft and nimble that results were most thorough, even though at first they required instruction in the use of materials with which they were not familiar.

This structure, designed theoretically and worked out practically to withstand distortion or fracture by earthquake, was put to the test while nearing completion in April, 1922, in broad daylight, during the heaviest temblor in point of severity Japan has known in fifty years. Wide destruction was wrought in the city of Tokyo. The shock was terrific. The Imperial was violently jolted. It visibly trembled, swayed and rocked in the upheaval, and at its ending quietly steadied to position, free of distortion, rents or damage of any kind.

So much for a system of construction altogether novel in conception and execution, carried out by a strong, persistent mind, as imaginative in its insight into fundamental principles of engineering as in its profound insight into the romance of breathing life and beauty, humanity and spirit, into forms and materials otherwise helplessly inert.

It is thus that the master mind works, to bring forth, out

of the fabric of a dream, a fabric of enduring reality. As to the interior, a noteworthy feature is the use of lava and brick in the grand promenade, the theatre, the restaurant and the banquet hall. It was a happy thought to penetrate the interior with materials of the exterior, thus giving a sense of enduring construction.

The equipment is thorough and complete; electric heating, light and motive power, the usual telephone service, and a system of mechanical ventilation constantly in use and so arranged as to deliver cooler air in summer.

All furniture, rugs and hangings of the public rooms are of special design, simple, strong and rich, partaking of the character and specifically related to the forms of the structure in a fine play of polychrome.

The guest room arrangement of the wings has been worked out to conserve space, concentrate conveniences and preserve a quiet effect. The rooms are not large, but are arranged and furnished to become sitting rooms; the beds are in evidence more as couches than as beds. The typical small room is 15 by 18, with a 6 by 10 bathroom deducted. The typical large room is 15 by 22, bathroom similarly deducted. Average ceiling height 9 feet 4 inches. The electric heating and indirect lighting are combined in a standard attached to twin tables in the center of each room. These tables have a small writing table and a small tea table beneath them which may be removed to any part of the room, and, when not in use, may be returned to their places as part of the central group. The electric heat is thus at the center of the room.

(For the rooms, see illustrations on page: 127, 128, 129). The wardrobe is a built-in feature of each bedroom, and is designed to accomodate a steamer trunk, a wardrobe trunk and two suit cases.

It has ample hanging space for clothes and the drawers of the old-fashioned dresser have been worked into this feature. There is storage space above it for purchases. A feature of this wardrobe is a guest-box accessible from the corridor or the bedroom at the will of the guest. This guest-box also contains the telephone.

A full length mirror is placed against the side wall, and a small dressing table placed beside it. The central group of tables and this dressing table, together with an overstuffed easy chair or two, a light, wooden chair or two, and a hassock, are all the furniture of the room, except the couch-beds. It will be seen in this arrangement that great simplicity has been arrived at. An individual color scheme characterizes each room. A specially designed rug to correspond is upon the floor. (For this Rug, see reproduction on page 105.)

The furniture covering, bed covers and window hangings are of the same stuff and color, and correspond in each case with the color note of the room. The color scheme ranges through the whole gamut of color from quiet grays to bright rose and old blue or gold.

The effect of the whole is quiet and complete. Everywhere there is ample light. Privacy is insured by the omission of the transom and the device of the guest-box. Cross-ventilation is secured in every room and bathroom by means of forced draught acting through ducts and a series of square ventilators set in the corridor partition above the picture rail. These are easily adjusted for summer or winter use.

The corridor ceilings are all dropped beneath the concrete slabs to make continuous ducts, to which are connected the vertical vent shafts between every pair of rooms. These vertical shafts extend from basement to attic space and contain pipes and wiring, which are accessible and free of the construction everywhere. The bathroom is an adjunct of the bedroom; in every case treated as a part of it. It is lined with ivory colored mosaic tiles, all external and internal corners curved. The bathtub is a sunken pool in the floor of the room, formed, with curved corners, of the same mosaic tile as the floor and the walls. The room has a vaulted ceiling, and screened windows in the outer wall. The whole is drained and impervious to water in every part. The floor is electrically heated from below.

The main corridors of the guest wings are six feet wide, exposing the brick-faced concrete piers that support

the floor, giving to the whole the effect of a cloistered promenade. The corridors are artificially lighted through perforated metal screens set into the ceiling.

The corridor floors are cork-tiled. The threshold has everywhere been eliminated. Where plaster has been used the walls are treated with ground pearl shell splashed on to a heavy coat of paint in the Japanese manner. All the windows in the building are screened, shaded and curtained. The wood, where used in the trimming, is throughout of Hokkaido oak, waxed. Outside each large room is a tiled balcony or terrace reached by low windows opening upon it. Baggage rooms, in each wing, for the storage of guests' luggage, easily accessible at any time, are located next to the elevators on the general level.

Thus an attempt has been made by this writer to set forth as clearly as may be the nature of a great work of architectural art founded in this particular case upon the utilities associated with human needs, in its aspects of hotel life and administration; or, in another sense, the forms that have been caused by a luminous thought to arise in sublimated expression of these needs in visible forms of beauty.

The true meaning of the word p r a c t i c a l is completely elucidated in this structure. For "practical" signifies explicit and implicit human needs. Such needs run a wide gamut of desire, ranging from the immediately physical and material, gradually upward in series through the desires of emotional, intellectual and spiritual satisfactions.

Thus we can understand how important is the play of imagination; for imagination is distinct from intellect. It lies deeper in life, and uses intellect as a critical executive instrument wherewith to carry its visions of reality into reality itself, while determining its quality of procedure, at every stage. Otherwise intellect would dominate imagination, and pervert its ends.

Thus what we call art and what we call science are indissoluble within a masterful imagination. But imagination must be free to act in true accord with need and with desire as fundamental human traits; and intellect must be disciplined by the will to act in accord with imagination's fine desires. But for this initiative, and to this end, man's spirit must be free: unimpeded by irrelevant inhibitions. The vision of the free spirit ever seeks to clarify, to amplify what we call the commonplace. It sees within the so-called commonplace the elements of sublimity. Thus the architect who combines in his being the powers of vision, of imagination, of intellect, of sympathy with human need and the power to interpret them in a language vernacular and true — is he who shall create poems in stone, consonant with the finer clearing thought of our day, and the days of our expectancy.

In this regard the Imperial Hotel stands unique as the high water mark thus far attained by any modern architect. Superbly beautiful it stands — a noble prophecy.

□   □   □

REFLECTIONS ON THE TOKYO ☐ ☐ DISASTER ☐ ☐ BY LOUIS H. SULLIVAN ☐ 1924

In my preceding article on the Imperial Hotel in Tokyo I prefaced by saying:

"On the vast stage of the world drama, two ideas. both of them immense in power, confront each other in spectacular appeal to the fears and the courage of mankind." The casual reader, as a rule, is not accustomed to those generalizations which go under the — to him — somewhat repellent name of philosophy, and in so far as philosophy has dealt and deals solely with abstractions and nonentities, he is right in his disdain — which I share. Such philosophies as have gone by the names Platonic, Neo-Platonic, and German Transcendentalism, have done their huge share to fill the world with sorrow, for they and their kind are the intellectual basis of tyranny. And this same casual reader is as casually apt to be unaware that day by day he lives under the tyranny of abstract dehumanized ideas; that he is under the dominion of ideas he had no share in making, ideas so diaphanous and all-pervading that they are as the air he breathes. His disdain of philosophy therefore is but disdain of a w o r d. Of the saturnine content of that word he is as unsuspecting as a kitten. If he is a university man, an aspirant in philosophy, he has been taught to revere that word and its content; and in innocence he reveres them both — and so another kitten, not in the least comprehending the utter heartlessness of it all; not in the least perceiving in the world about him the corruption and dislocation that have followed in its train. To be sure there are readers and readers. One reads

industriously, and learns nothing — he is credulous. Another reads industriously and learns nothing — he is cynical. Another reads even more industriously and widely and learns nothing — he is pessimistic. But of all three and their varieties, the credulous one is in the most pitiful plight.

He may read the philosophies of abstraction and find them ennobling, he may believe himself to be lifted up and to have entered the highest attainable domain of pure thought — the realm of the ideal, the perfect, the absolute, in which the intellect reigns supreme — regarding itself in its own supernatural mirror, its gaze fatefully turned away from man and from his world. And of such belief in the unreal is the basis for all credulity — especially in evidence in the wool-gathering highbrow. Yet there is another class of reader — he who regards not authority, eminence, nor prestige as finalities, but who seeks that which nourishes and enlarges his comprehension of life, and who, therefore, as by instinct of self-preservation, rejects that which sterilizes life — that is to say the abstract. To him therefore Life becomes an ever broadening, deepening, sublimating and impressive flow, within which he finds himself moving — his own life unfolding, and with the passing years thus arises, within, a deep religious and moral sympathy with the vast spectacle of immediate life, enfolding mankind, which he envisages as participant and spectator. In sympathy there arises within, a new pity allied to a new faith in man.

With spontaneous gesture the newly-arising philosophy, with the voice of which I speak, sweeps aside the spooks and phantasms which have tyrannized the credulous and made slaves of high and low, even in our own day of so-called enlightenment, and with mind thus

cleared for action and merging with the flow of life seeks therein a comprehension of mankind, in order to arrive at an outline of conservation, which, in its directness of purpose, may supersede the abominable wastage of humanity due to the prevailing confusion of ideas.

In one aspect the eye views an incredibly frantic industry, with no objective but to s e l l, and in another aspect — an inexorable reaction of the first — a steady decline in thought beyond the immediate frenzy, a terrifying inability to foresee the consequences of a thought or an act; or worse, a wanton and brutal disregard. And while it is a fact that the thoughts here above set down arise immediately out of contemplation of the helplessness, the shabbiness, the ruthless debauchery of commercialized American architecture — which means death — the same thought reaches out over the world and crossing the wide waters arrives at Japan with its city of Tokyo, in which has been staged, as but yesterday, a startling tragedy of ideas, wherein the abstract has crumbled in universal ruin, while one l i v i n g thought and living thing survives. This is what is involved in the significance of the statement that on the vast stage of the world-drama two ideas, both of them immense in power, confront each other in spectacular appeal to the fears and the courage of mankind.

The emergence, unharmed, of the Imperial Hotel, from the heartrending horrors of the Tokyo disaster, takes on, at once, momentous importance in the world of modern thought, as a triumph of the living and the real over the credulous, the fantastic and the insane.

It emerges moreover before our gaze as an imposing upreared monument to the power of common sense; to that consummate common sense which perceives, comprehends, and grasps the so-called commonplace, the real, as distinct from the abstract; to that common sense which founds its logic upon the power inhering in nature's processes, when interpreted in terms of action, as affecting results; soundly scientific in foreseeing results; and which towards this end employs an accurate imagination. For it requires unusual imagination to see stone as stone, brick as brick, wood as wood, steel as steel, the earth as the earth and human beings as human beings.

We may call this power Inspiration if we please, and if we think the word sounds pleasanter than Philosophy.

But it is well to bear in mind that Inspiration is philosophy in its highest estate, and that true philosophy is systemized common sense in its finest human reach.

□   □   □

In planning the erection of a structure in a terrain habitually given to earthquake it would seem to be natural to regard earthquake — otherwise seismic disturbance — as a fundamental. For earthquakes are not imaginary or abstract or illusory; they are real — and at times calamitous. It would seem, therefore, to be but the part of common sense not to invite destruction. Yet such is the pervading American credulity, such its inability to think straight; such its impulsive acceptance of "go-gettism" and "pep" and "progress" and "enterprise" as substitutes for reflection and sound thought, and social responsibility, that it succeeded by sales-methods in imposing upon the Japanese, structures so childish, so absurd, so uncomprehending, as verily to invite destruction. To be sure the Japanese themselves were credulous enough to take the bait of boosted land values, and multiplied areas; and in their cupidity were induced to hold the bag. When the time came they found the bag filled not with purring kittens, but with terrifying wild-cats.

Prior to the American invasion, there has been an English invasion; and prior to the English, a German invasion, both invasions carrying with them the sophisticated credulity of European culture. Both of these alien cultures erected solid masonry buildings upon earthquake land. When the time came, these structures groaned, and buried their dead.

Now, further, Japanese society being heaviest at the top, it would seem but in keeping that its indigenous structures, designed in the native idiom, built on narrow and tortuous lanes, should also be topheavy. When the time came the flying heavy roof tiles did their share in the general slaughter, and as well the flimsy bridges and the flimsiness in general. Thus ruined Tokyo became the prey of conflagration. Thus death arose out of the temblor and spread forth its arms over Tokyo doomed by a false premise.

It may seem quite easy to draw conclusions after the fact. If you really think so, try your hand on the European war. Or, make a diagnosis of contemporary American architecture. Or attempt an analysis of the American mind, tracing its activities back to their com-

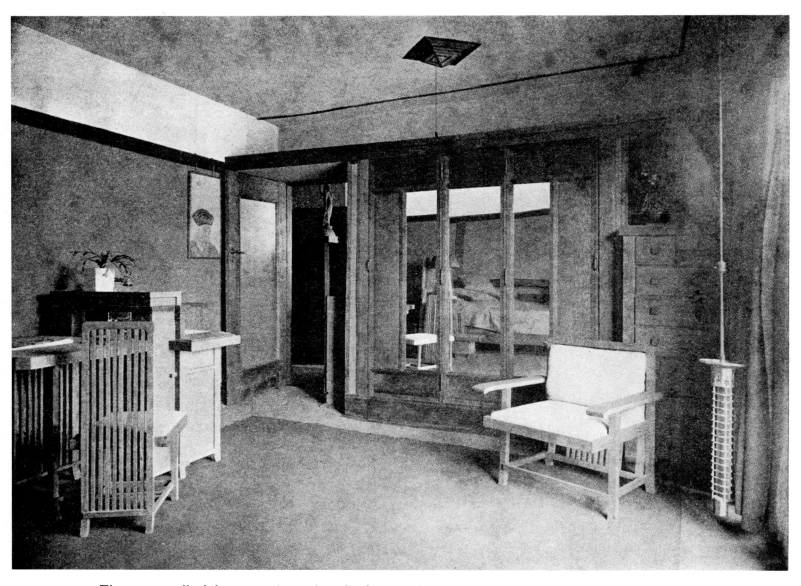

mon source. These are, all of them, matters after the fact.

□　　　　　□　　　　　□

We are now to deal with the reverse aspect of the problem. That is to say, with the primary assumption of earthquake and disaster, and how to forefend. Some five years prior to the now historic temblor a young man of forty seven was called to Tokyo to consult as architect regarding the planning and construction of a great hotel to be called the "Imperial". This man, a poet, who had reduced thinking to simples, began his solution with the fixed fact of earthquakes as a basis and made an emotional study of their nature and movements. The second move was the resolve never to relax his grip on the basis fact of earthquake as a menace, and to devise a system of construction such as should absorb and dispose of the powerful shocks, waves and violent tremors, and yet maintain its integrity as a fabricated structure. It may be remarked in passing, that the quality and power of emotion dramatizes the power of thought; that the poet is he whose thought, thus enriched, imparts telling power to the simple and the obvious, bringing them into the field of vivid cons-

ciousness.

It is precisely this power of the poet to bring earthquake vividly into consciousness and hold it there, that distinguishes him, in this instance, from the uninspired engineer. The latter is an extremely useful person, wherever and whenever his formulas, his slide-rule, his tables and his precedents — to which he is a slave — apply. Within the limits of routine he may successfully vary his processes in application; and there his social value ends. The same, in substance, may be said of the uninspired practicing architect, except that the latter, in addition, is invertebrate. Wherever he thinks with reasonable clearness, he approaches the engineer; but he is not a Yea-Sayer — he prefers to trim. Yet the great creative engineer — and there have been such — by virtue of clear eyesight, material realization and the power to dream, is again the poet if he fail not in the human sense of beauty, even though he may not think so, and out of prudence may not say so. Yet he is essentially of the Yea-Sayers — and the Yea-Sayers are the great modern poets.

The architect of the Imperial Hotel, whose name by

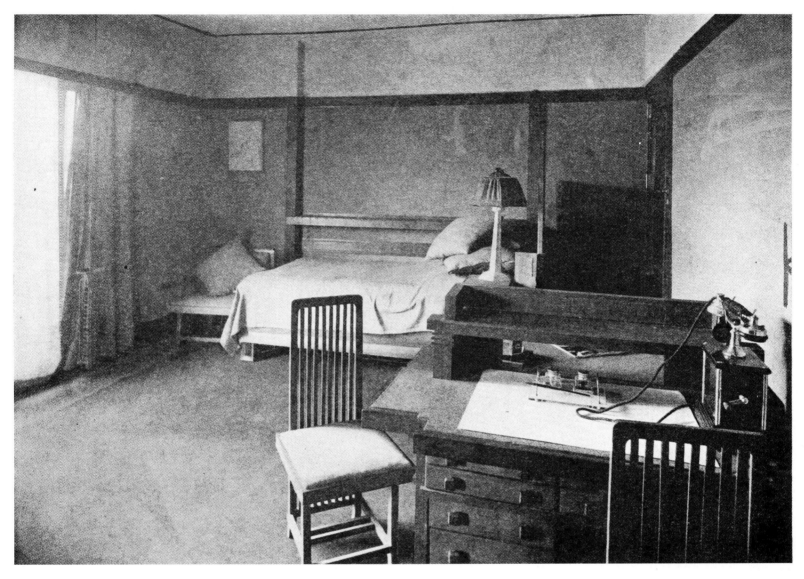

the way is Frank Lloyd Wright, a fact I should in all honor have mentioned earlier, had I not been so engrossed in an attempt to clothe in words the basic idea of my thesis — the most dangerous and destructive of all ideas — the idea of Credulity; this architect I say, whom I have known since his eighteenth year, and the workings of whose fine mind I believe I fairly follow, is possessed of a rare sense of the human, and an equally rare sense of Mother Earth, coupled with an apprehension of the material, so delicate as to border on the mystic, and yet remain coördinate with those facts we call real life. Such mind, sufficiently enriched by inner experiences as to become mellow in power, and reinforced by a strong tenacious will, is precisely the primary type of mind that resolves a problem into its simples, and out of these simples projects in thought a masterful solution, and in the process of transmuting thought into actual material fact, displays a virtuosity in the manipulation of the simples of technique.

I admit it is difficult for a mind academically trained and hence in large measure deprived of its freedom and its natural susceptibility, to grasp an idea so foreign to its heritage of tradition as is, necessarily so, the idea of simples. I go further and assert that such idea may be repugnant to such minds — may even alarm such minds — it is too disturbing in its ominous suggestion that thoughts may be living things — Now! — Here! — The intrusion of Life upon such minds may indeed be disheartening. And the same statements may apply with equal force to the mind technically trained exclusively — the world of life shut out; and as well to the business mind, with its airy system of phantasies, its curious rules of the game, its pontifical utterances of the higher wisdom of mendacity, and its one, solid, credulous faith in the abstract notion, deeply cherished, that human life is and must ever be a battle, a struggle for existence, and thus believing render itself "the unfit" to analyze its own symptoms which predicate periodical collapse of the structure it has reared upon the soil of an earthquake thought. And yet, in contrast, the open mind which may have won its freedom through valor, going forth into the world of men and thoughts and things, discerns basic simples everywhere and in all things. To such mind the confusion of the world is no mystery.

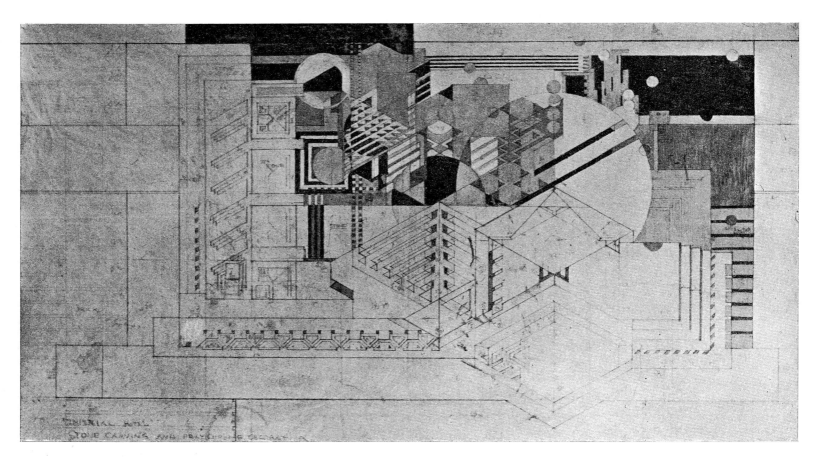

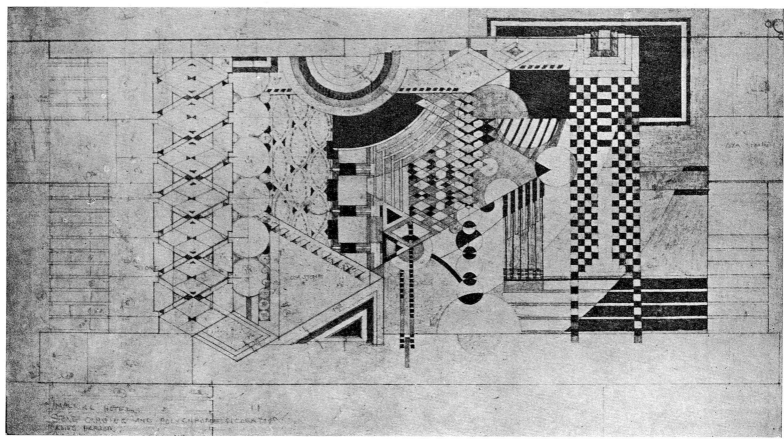

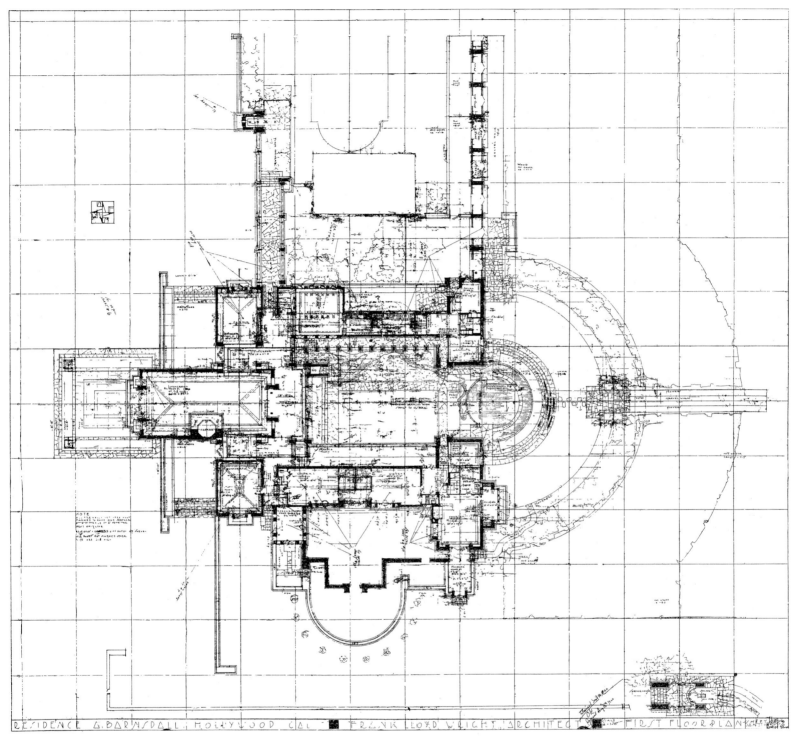

It is no part of my business here, nor of my intent, to go into the technical refinements, the subtleties of re-action, and the plastic sense of balance and free move-ment that enter into the structural theory and actuality of the Imperial Hotel. Mr. Wright may do this if he so sees fit. The vast sumptuous building, in all its aspects: structural, utilitarian and aesthetic, was the embodiment, and is now the revelation, of a single thought tenaciously held by a seer and a prophet, a craftsman, a master-builder.

This most significant architectural monument that the modern world can show, stands today uninjured because it was thought-built, so to stand. It was not and is not an imposition upon the Japanese, but a free will contri-bution to the finest elements of their culture. The fame of the building and its author is now world-wide; and we will let it go at that.

Meanwhile, I declare as my real business and my true intent herein, to be that of one of enquiring mind who seeks in this disaster the realities behind its terrifying mask.

FACTS REGARDING THE IMPERIAL HOTEL FIRST.
The New Imperial is a hotel of solid masonry construction containing commodious public rooms and 285 bedrooms together with 225 outside bathrooms. This much however is less than one-half its substance, or its function, or its cost.

It is also a centre of entertainment — a clearing house for Japan's social obligations to "the foreigner" and this group contains the 300 foot masonry promenade with 16 private supper rooms — a masonry theatre with revolving stage. In the theatre there are one thousand seats. There is below the theatre a terraced cabaret seating at tables 300 people with dancing space and stage. Above the theatre is the banquet hall with capacity to seat a thousand at table. A gallery is continued all around it. Like the theatre, it too is done in imperishable materials, — a great building in itself. Group I, the hotel, would cost anywhere in America at least two million dollars, probably much more — f u r n i s h e d.

Group II, the entertainment group would cost two and a half million dollars at least, anywhere in the U.S.A. The Imperial Hotel, f u r n i s h e d, cost 20 % less per Tsubo than any building in Tokyo erected under foreign influence durlng the past five years has cost, u n f u r-n i s h e d. There are 10,400 Tsubo of actual free floor space in this building, excluding terraces and gardens. A Tsubo is 36 square feet.

SECOND. The ceiling heights, of the typical bedrooms average 9'—4", they vary slightly in the different stories. The typical small guest room is 15×18 feet with a 6×10 bathroom included in the outside fore corner. The typical large room is 15×22 with a 6×10 bathroom included in the outside fore corner.

There are many larger rooms en suite. Some of them 36'0" wide. Each room has ample glass surface as any truthful occupant will testify — summer or winter. The rooms and bathrooms are all outside rooms opening on gardens or streets.

If we study the building method of Italy or other semi-tropical nations we find thick walls — small openings

and rather high ceilings, — high ceilings because there was no forced draught used in former times. High ceilings in Japan, wich has a climate of extremes work both ways — for comfort in summer — dead against it in winter, because heating is very expensive in Japan. The cool chambers protected by the masses of the masonry itself is the best protection against heat of the sun. And provided the air is kept circulating from the coolest places from which it can be taken and delivered from beneath the roof surfaces to the outside air the best has been done that could be done for comfort in humid hot weather.

This is the design of the Imperial and the means taken to work it out have gone more thoroughly into the matter and the system is more complete than in any other modern building known.

THIRD. The "stone" is a lava called OYA. It is the "stone ordinaire" of Japan. It is indestructible by water or fire. It will not disintegrate — it is not to be penetrated by moisture. When first quarried it is soft and easily workable. It hardens on exposure to the weather and turns yellow. I found buildings with arrises still sharp and clean that had been standing 35 years; saw it where it has been underground for 70 years. It weighs 96 pounds per cubic foot — about the weight of green oak.

It is cupped by pockets of burned wood left as the lava flowed down over fhe forests. It is an ideal building stone similar to Travertine or Caen but with finer character than either. I would be content to have it and no other for the rest of my life as a medium with which to build. Because it was so easily worked I could hollow it out and use it for forms into which the concrete slabs cantilevers or walls were cast and the steel reinforcement be tied into the joints as well as hooked into the material from beneath and all cast solidly together with the concrete. Wherever there was a chance for a flaked off piece, copper was used in connection with it to insure it.

No terra cotta — no stones — could furnish the same

security as this lava for the features of the building in an earthquake country.

The proof of this came with the earthquake in April 1922. This was the most severe earthquake in Japan for 52 years and there was no check nor crack nor fallen piece in the finished construction anywhere. Next day the building was visited by architects, societies, insurance companies and others and the facts here stated may easily be verified. This work was done under the constant personal supervision of Mr. Mueller.

Exceptions taken to this free use of lava as a plastic material were silenced by the earth quake.

FOURTH. In the erection of the New Imperial Parliament Buildings, the scheme of foundation originally designed for the Imperial Hotel has been adopted.

In the original design I had intended to bore the holes for the concrete piles but owing to the fact that old piles and stones abounded in the soil Mr. Mueller found it more advantageous to punch the holes with a wooden tapered pile. This system of foundation saved my clients hundreds of thousands of dollars over the usual system; but more important than that, I believe it to be the

logical system for any earthquake country, or a soft ground locality like Chicago or Tokyo. This foundation was undertaken in the interest of my clients, carefully, after many preliminary tests extending over a period of a year or more — with full knowledge of all that the matter entailed. Apparently an old subterranean water course took its way diagonally across the building lot in a streak about twenty feet wide and made itself felt in the building as it went up — but the natural means of reinforcement which was part of the original design known as "the reserve" was employed. And I was enabled to increase heights or weights after the foundations were in by employing the same means with no greater expense than had it been put in in the first place.

The scientific basis, tests and figures upon which this foundation was put in will sometime be put on record by myself.

Levels taken with an instrument a day or two after the terrible quake of April 1922 showed no deviation whatever of the footings by seismic disturbance anywhere throughout the vast length and breadth of the great structure.

Only a tyro in building would spend his clients money to avoid the natural squeeze to the extent of several inches on ground like that on which the Imperial stands. The entire foundation was intended to settle to this extent; and such settlement was provided for.

FIFTH. The swimming pool is tile-lined and purified by violet rays.

As a temporary engineering expedient — I retained the water in the tank; construction completed the tank may be pumped out or in at will.

All gravel walks or drives are temporary only. OYA pavements are everywhere where people tread on the ground outside the building.

SIXTH. The masonry Theatre has seats for one thousand people. It has four 5'6" pairs of doors opening to two stairway halls directly accessible and reaching as directly the garden at the rear.

It has also four pairs of doors 5'6" wide on the main floor and balcony opening to the 300 foot masonry promenade. Two more exits 8'0" wide are provided in the balcony opening to the promenade balcony or adjoining terraces. At the rear of all of these balconies, swinging windows open to adjacent fireproof rooms or terraces. The theatre is a "grotto" sculptured out of stone cast into the structure as an integral part of it. There is nothing to burn except the backs of the seats and there is nothing "suspended" in it. It is safer than any stucco interior could possibly be.

And here a word concerning the splay and cantilever construction which I have adopted in this building throughout. The cantilever in reinforced concrete construction, when it is an extension of a continuous slab, affords a reaction that makes wide spans economically possible, balances weights over centers instead of leaving them to grasp at the sides of walls and affords scientifically the overhanging projections which here make the novice nervous. In this building the cantilever is a principle of construction as free and romantic in fact as is the conception of the whole in form.

For an earthquake country it is an ideal system because the tremor of superimposed loads is centered squarely and fairly on supports. In a change I desired to make, the resistance to destruction of one of the larger overhangs was almost incredible.

As used in this structure it is worthy of study for its own sake. It is a new element that means a new form of Architecture.

Reality is no more to be set aside in Architecture than in other expressions of human thought and feeling. Great Art is an inner experience, coming to few, but what constitutes Truth in Art is one with Truth in Life. A seemingly insane world fights cruel battles to defend the foolish "Rituals" that continually confuse it. By egotism Man is pushed further and further from o r i g i n s, from inner "experience" until the voice of Principle sounds far away to him if heard at all. Truth is costly, it too, is an inner "experience". It can not be labeled, pigeon-holed or made into rituals and live. The modern Renaissance is a ritual and doomed.

Throughout it's length and breadth the New Imperial is a thoroughbred — a great building grown great in rugged native materials built for and by and in the land in which it stands and tied in with its Traditions. No light matter! What could one of Belshazzar's slaves know about a thing like that? Let him call a Daniel.

It is an Architect's tribute to a unique nation he has loved. Nor is one single utilitarian feature deserted in this Imperial Guest House — they are the very features of the whole. One may at first not like them — but if one has studied Architecture as a scientific Art and not merely accepted it as a Salesmans formula or a recipe for cooking — then the harmonious organic nature of the whole will, in time, please, edify — thrill, I say, and one may conscientiously and consistently endorse it as truly and splendidly sane. Light and shade play lovingly with the patterned, fretted overhanging cornices sifting patterned sun-splashes on strudy walls, tempering but not obstructing the light. A true and simple gaiety. No other building seems to have this charming grace caught from foliage overhead in a wood or from pine branches overhanging a road.

Yet with all its grace and modernity, the Imperial has the strength of the primitive — it harks back to origins. The quality of the Imperial, as the Japanese say, is "shibui" — meaning a thing at first disliked, coming back again — interested, back again — beginning to see, and ten times revisited — loved. We have no such word. It refers to a quality in a thing that asserts itself as beauty only when one has grown to it.

There is the strength of Joy in the forms of the Impe-

rial — the joy of strength — standing square and sturdy on their mud cushion against impending earth-quakes. One may not like them — at first, but go again and see and then go again and again.

SHIBUI! A mysterious, quiet, — deep in the Oriental Soul beneath the Oriental surface, — fruit of an experience ages older than any culture the Occident yet knows. These United States could crawl on suppliant knees to breathe its spirt and be ennobled by it. Nothing in our gift can equal this in their's — this treasure of the humble seeking reality.

The Imperial stands true to the spirit of old Japan, it speaks a truth slumbering in those ancient depths; it is true in itself to the work it was meant to do: to shelter, give aid, comfort and entertainment to Japan's guests. It is refreshing to seekers after Truth because it has been ennobled by the strength of the primitive. The Imperial is a building not for apologists — but for enquirers, not for fakirs busy with superficial taste and morality, but for seekers of evidence of the vital creative power of Man. In the Imperial the Art of Architecture comes to grips with reality for the sake of a better order. It has no quarrel with life as lived now, but belongs at the present time to the more advanced stage of culture because it insists upon every utilitarian need as an ordered thing in a harmonious whole. It is a conservation of space, energy and time by concentration and the invention of practical ways and means to this end. This is just such conservation as existed in old Japan. That selfsame principle is here at work and should help the Japanese to re-establish that wonderful thing in the new life that appears inevitable to them. The Imperial is the first great protest against the Guargantuan waste adopted by Japan from the old German precedents when there were no better ones. Since then the world has moved with incredible rapidity. Conservation of space by concentrated conveniences has gone far. The ship began it, the Pullman car took it up, the Ocean Liner went further and now the modern Hotel, on costly ground, is at work upon it. The element that enjoyed the license of the old never-to-be-heated waste space, — the element that obliterated everything with a freight car load of luggage — put its feet up on the table and spit on the floor as regardless of environment as a horse in a stable, just so the bedding was there and the feed and water handy — won't like the Imperial at first, — some of them never will.

□   □   □

BARNSDALL THEATRE, OLIVE HILL

BARNSDALL THEATRE, OLIVE HILL

LOS ANGELOS CALIFORNIA (SECOND PLAN)

LOS ANGELOS CALIFORNIA (FIRST PLAN)

BARNSDALL
RESIDENCE
HOLLYWOOD
CALIFORNIA
AND GENERAL
□ PLAN OF □
BARNSDALL
□ THEATRE □

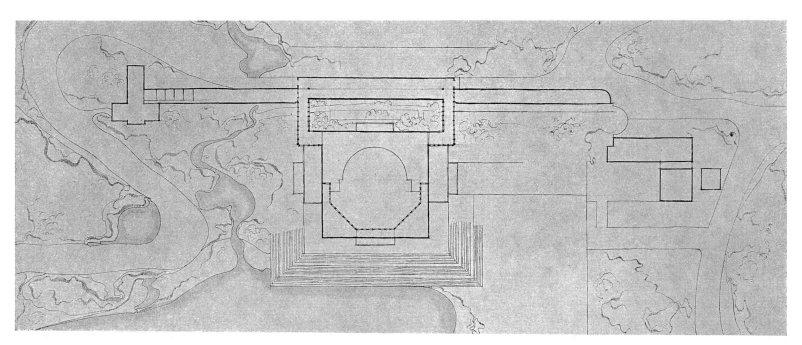

BARNSDALL
RESIDENCE
HOLLYWOOD
CALIFORNIA
□ AND STUDY □
PERSPECTIVE
BARNSDALL
□ THEATRE □

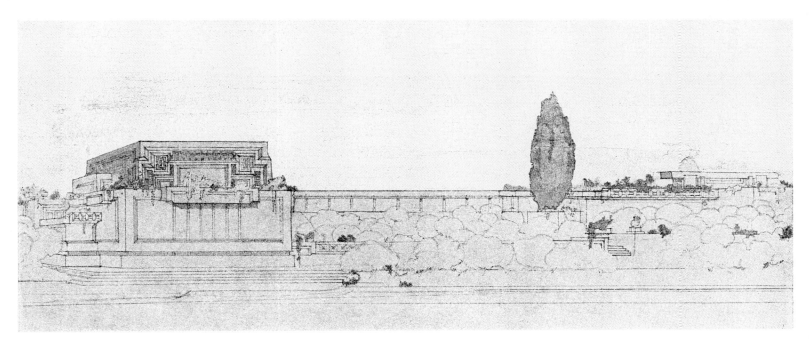

147

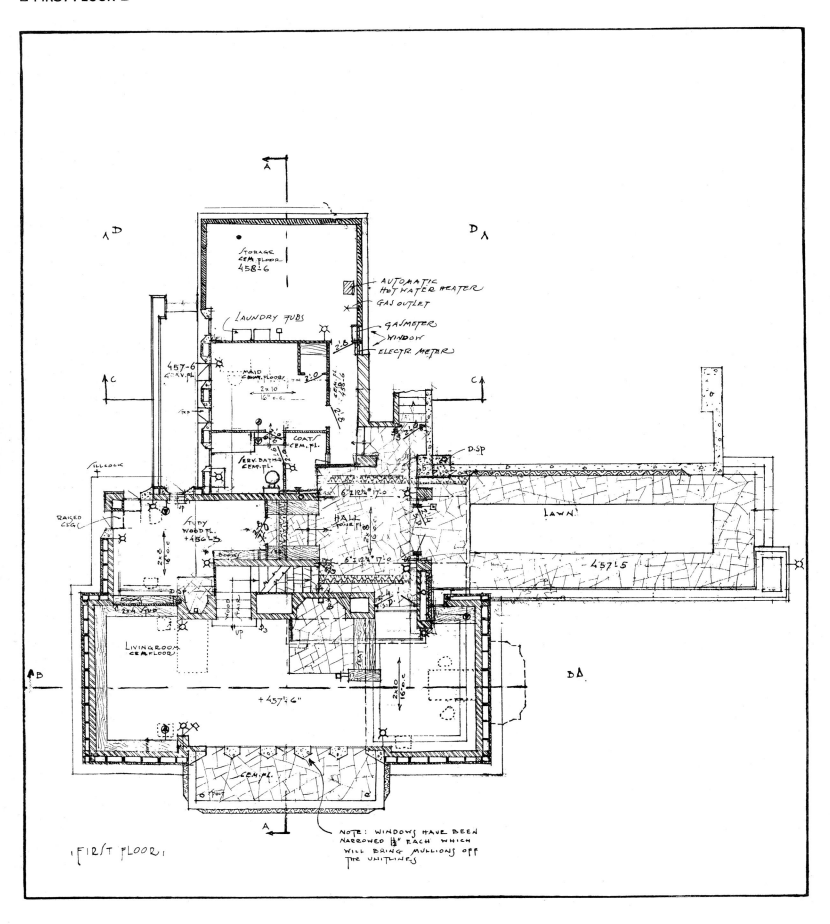

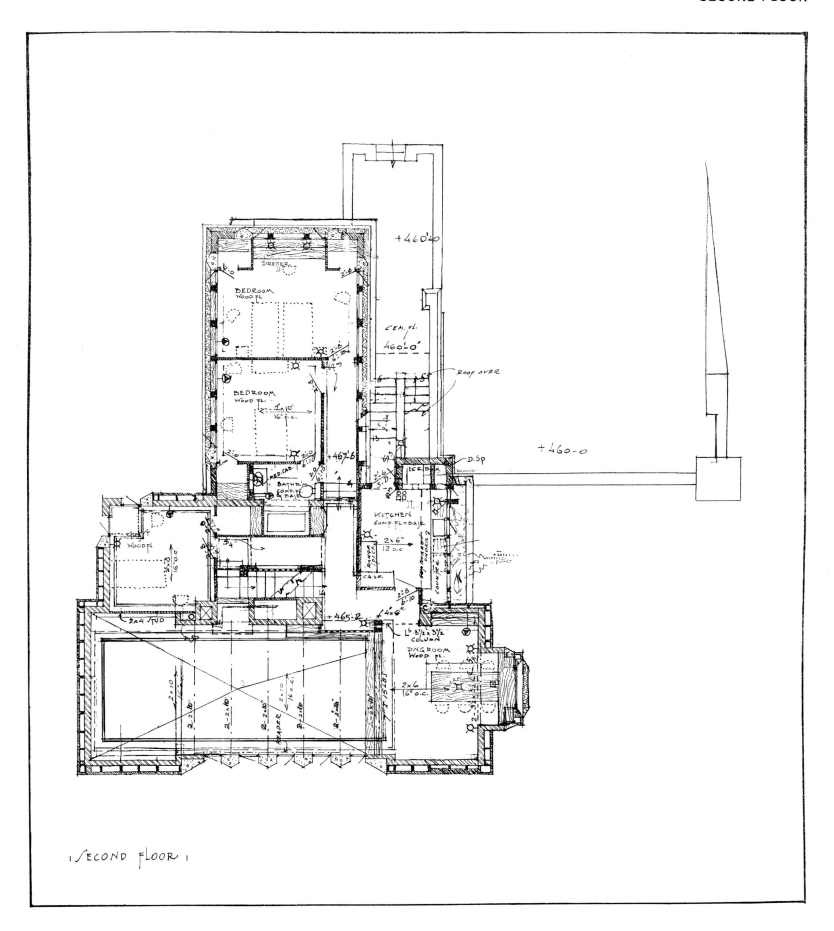

ı SECOND FLOOR ı

RESIDENCE "B" OLIVE HILL

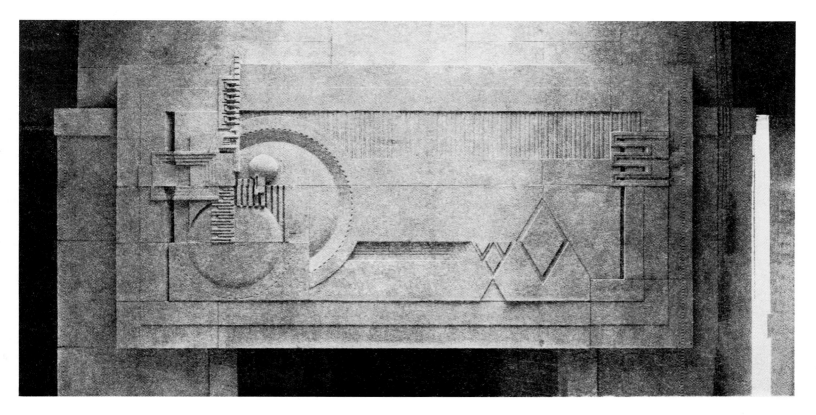

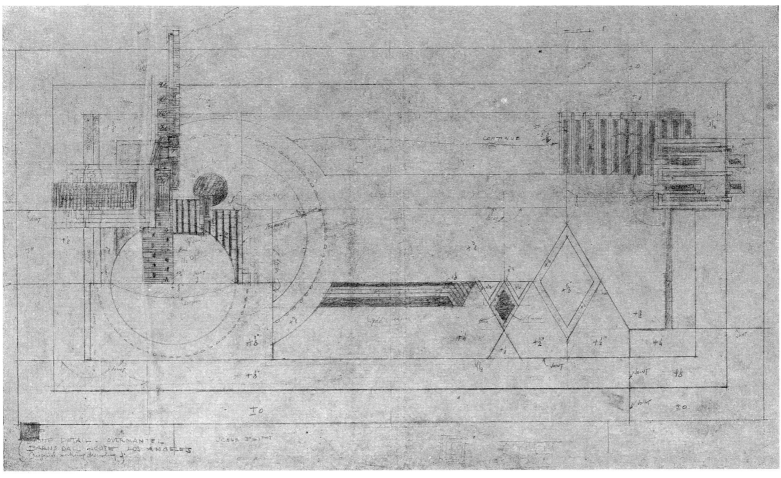

□ BARNSDALL □
□ RESIDENCE □
HOLLYWOOD
LONGITUDINAL
□ SECTION OF □
□ THEATRE □

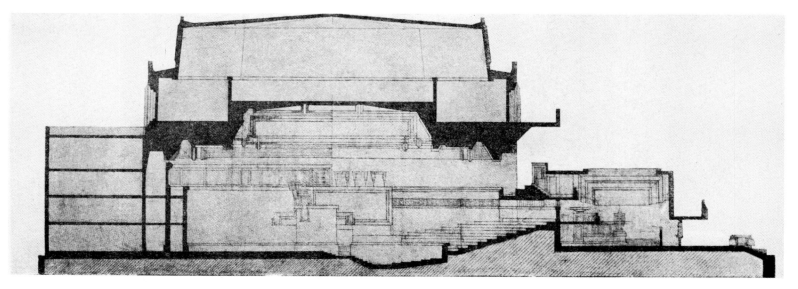

□ BARNSDALL □
□ RESIDENCE □
HOLLYWOOD
AND SECTION
□ OF THEATRE □
TOWARDS REAR

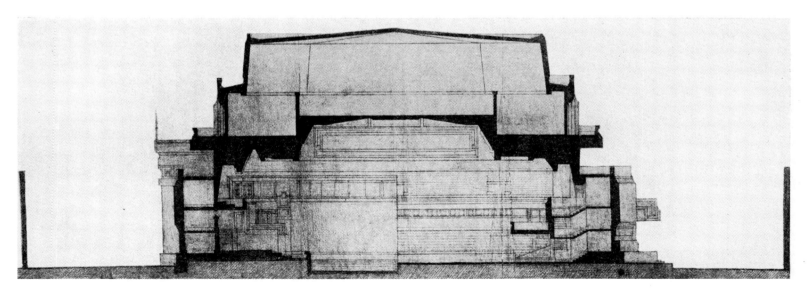

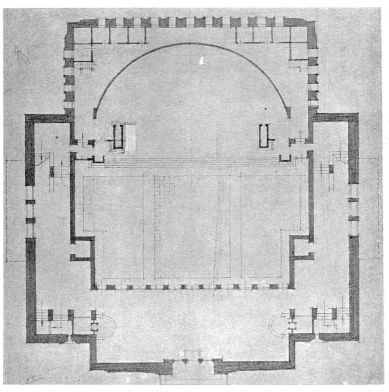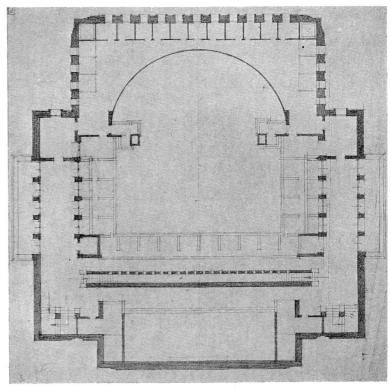

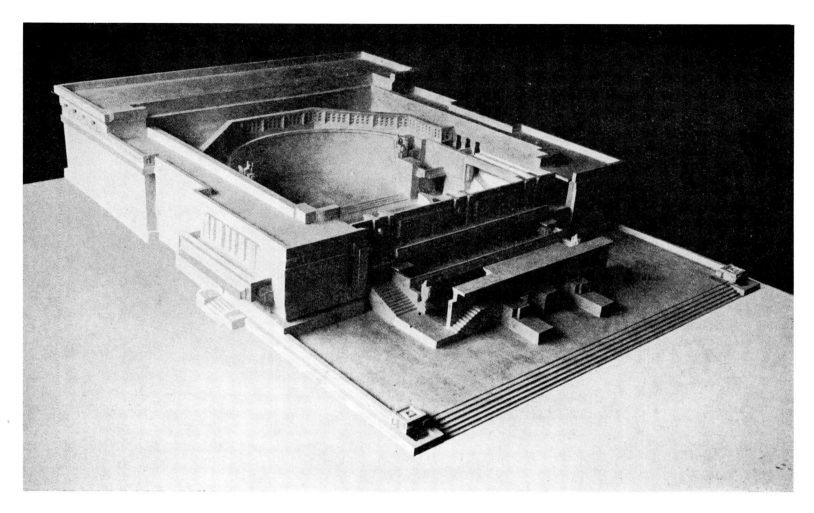

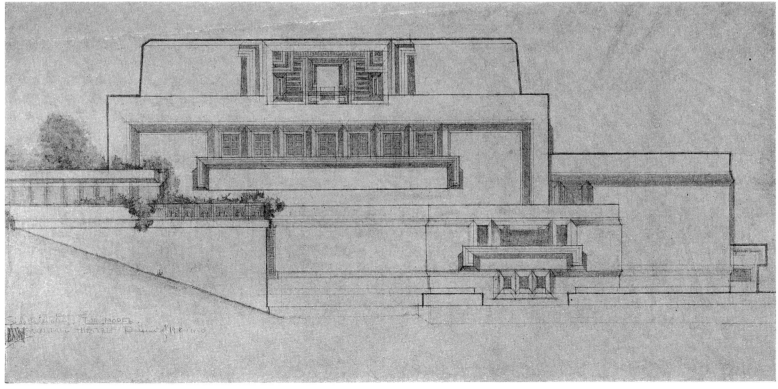

TO MY EUROPEAN CO-WORKERS
BY FRANK LLOYD WRIGHT

Heer Wijdeveld asks me for a message to my co-workers of the "old-world". I who am of this alleged "new-world" that is America, see this new-world among you, as I see your alleged old-world in this one — and we all seem to desire much the same thing. Although we may phrase our sense of it differently or seek it in different ways, it is true that some Principle is working in us to get something, — or maybe itself only, — born, and we are the happy or anguished victims of its purpose as the case may be.

This seems material enough for infinite miracles.

The tree lives and fulfills its destiny, its "design" inevitably. The life-principle of the tree seems fixed and simple. Ours is really as simple though perhaps more flowing, and it is a song in our hearts, the Symphony of Nature. The song is seldom heard clearly even by those who yearn most sincerely and take most pains to hear it. It is like beautiful music in another room heard now faintly and now more distinctly as the door, for some reason unknown to us, opens or again closes as we listen. Nevertheless this Principle that makes the music and that we sometimes, according to habit, call Man or Truth or Love, will have its way with us — all of us, new in old, or old in new, and we serve. We become as that Man-principle wills and we are all one in effect as we are infinite in variety. Nothing we make as creative artists is ever wholly lost if when we made it we have listened well enough to hear the music in what we do. This thing we call Happiness is our sense of action when we are touched or moved by Truth, nothing more or less, indefinite or ephemeral though it may appear. Every work of art is a great deed — and the "thought" in it, the highest form of Action. In this Action we truly live and — are compelled to seek. So we artists live many lives and die as many deaths, eternally perhaps.

We become greater in service to the general effect, more harmonious a part of the whole — the "Universal" as we call it, as we coincide with the nature of Principle and the Principles of what we call Nature.

Meantime we communicate by means of signs, Symbols — and we too are in a sense ourselves no more than faulty Symbols as we do so; unwilling Symbols of Reality; feeble signs of the Principle, the Song of which we — by our intent listening are learning to sing.

Any letter or numeral is a sign. A word is a symbol. Paintings, sculpture, poems or buildings are all symbols. Institutions, Manners, Customs, Traditions, good or bad, all are but the residuum of "Living" — to become debris left stranded upon the shores of time as life recedes or goes from them entirely, further on, perhaps.

Sun, Moon and Stars are Symbols — Matter, no more than a symbol of what is living Spirit within. So it is natural we should regard Life as the one thing of value, and keep the life in our Symbols as expressions of Spirit — throwing them aside when they become useless or insignificant — burying them respectfully if there is need and time.

The "General effect", or "universe" or "organic whole" of life is too vast for use to seize in our imaginations — nor is it necessary to so grasp it. To fret concerning Cause or Purpose is as wise as was the boy who cut out the head of his drum to see where the sound came from. No creative artist ever does fret much about it — unless he falls sick and ceases to create and so loses direction.

We sense enough of the character of the "organic altogether" by five primitive senses made into a superior sixth, or, as we evolve, perhaps infinitely more, and we gain some healthy knowledge by rightly feeling our relationship to it. That feeling we call Love. When it takes form we call it Beauty. When the feeling is in action as creative-artist we call it intuitive-inspiration. When it is at work in this Love we call it Art. We grow to ever greater perception as we faithfully and gratefully cultivate life in this sense. Our civilization depends for its value upon that cultivation, as we say, "culture". In every faithful expression of this love of life in the work of making paintings, statues, books or buildings, or in other great deeds as expressions of Man, we grow in power to make greater likenesses, — to greater comprehension.

As seed in the earth responds to light in expanding to realization of life-principle, so we respond to this life-light which is within us and give birth to "Forms".

The growth of the Seed is a primitive symbol of our own growth, if we say Truth is Light or Love. Man makes a symbol for this light and calls it God. We cannot despise the Symbol just because reactionaries abuse it by using it as a thing of value in itself. When we try to discard it and soar in what seems a superior realm, we are probably sick with longing, or weary of pretense and stupidity, tired of waiting for something to happen; a nostalgia of the soul, it may be. But we are then unfruitful to humanity because we are untrue to the reality of ourselves and so uncreative in a form of living death. Death was given us not to use to arrest or destroy beauty — but, as the greatest German has said, that we might have more life. When we ourselves become abstractions we are lost — because then we are using the symbol as a thing in itself — abusing its privilege. We are "on" Life not "of" it — and betray our birthright inevitably. We ought to be "unhappy" and are, because we are inhuman, not fulfilling therefore, our "design", our destiny. We are drying in the ground if we are "Seeds"; the Sap is not running, we are not putting forth leaves if we are "trees"; we are not according to design, uncreative, if human beings.

Humanity has no "duty" toward the artist. The Artist none toward Humanity. It is all a matter of privilege on either side as a matter of course. It is a sense of privilege both need, rather than the sense of duty. Humanity is a quality, an element in all the artist does. He is that element incarnate.

Life itself is the supreme impulse as Artist and Living is the supreme work of art. And human beings? Faulty "Symbols" made to communicate meanwhile, in a process Love, Birth, Growth, and Decay: A procession privileged to play in and upon and to reflect the Idea that is Life. The artist is in no trance. — His dream finds its work and finds its mark in the Eternity that is Now. Life is concrete — each in each and all in all although our horizon may drift into mystery. In harmony with Principles of Nature and reaching toward Life-light, only so are we creative. By that Light we live, to become likewise. And all that need ever be painted or carved or built — are significant colorful shadows of that Light.

FRANK LLOYD WRIGHT AND THE NEW ARCHITECTURE

by Robert Mallet-Stevens, 1925

Modern architecture is not a vogue, it is a necessity. Modern architecture is not ornamental, it is useful and normal. Between the Rococo architecture of the Louis XV period and modern architecture there is the same difference as there is between a bedaubed carriage, laden with ornaments and shellwork from the "war of laces," and an automobile, with its smooth lines and streamlined forms. For centuries stone has been used for building. Every era has left its mark in stone, ornament alone defining a style, except for the Gothic style, in which the methods of construction influenced the esthetic aspect. If we go back to vehicles as an example, it is the same: a horse, shafts, a box, wheels; and these indispensable elements decorated in accordance with the taste and fashion of the moment. Suddenly everything changes: reinforced concrete appears and over-turns building procedures, the internal combustion engine replaces the horse. Science creates a new esthetics. Forms are extensively changed, the house and the car becoming funda-mentally different. There was an explanation for narrow, high window openings: stone does not allow the use of long lintels, and wide openings represented surfaces that ran the risk of making the interior cold. With reinforced concrete and central heating, the architect can distribute air and light through windows of enormous dimensions, and lintels can be length-ened. The exterior appearance of the house becomes totally different.

Cantilevers, thinner posts and jambs, and fewer points of support all combine to give the building a different feeling.

Only a few architects have understood the tremendous resources of reinforced concrete. Even though every builder now makes use of reinforced concrete, artists are still afraid to use new forms and their sluggish imagination prefers styles of the past.

Frank Lloyd Wright was one of the first to be adventurous, to break with a tradition bordering on routine, so that he could be creative. And his oeuvre is grand, rich, logical.

America, having no past (it must be said), had the right to select from among all the styles the one that best suited its needs, tastes and habits. In fact, only fifty years ago in America, a palace, an apartment building or a villa might be in the Gothic, Louis XVI or Empire style, with no one to object. When drawing inspiration from "past" styles of other, older countries, there was no reason to favor any one style over another. And I confess that an American skyscraper treated in the style of medieval monastic architecture was not much more ridiculous than a European railroad station built in Louis XVI style.

Then reinforced concrete arrived. Americans shunned that method of construction for quite some time; iron was pre-dominant in the building arts. Nevertheless, American engi-neers were constructing splendid factories. Certain industrial buildings are extremely beautiful; one can sense a clean, clear program, a sensible, economical conception and a conse-quently pursued logic—all giving a very pleasant esthetic result. It is a true and sincere architecture.

Wright, without drawing inspiration from any fashion of the past, saw and knew these buildings endowed with original lines (and theirs was not the originality that consists of systematically doing the opposite of what is customarily seen, but the originality resulting from the solution of a problem different from those hitherto proposed), Wright was surrounded by these sensible buildings. We Europeans, cut off from all experi-ment for a century (except for the Eiffel Tower), might say that his task was easier than ours! We architects of the Old World had to demolish the ornamental hotchpotch of the nineteenth century in a hostile atmosphere; before we could think of creating something new, we had to do away with the excessive and arbitrary ornamentation of that whole era of plagiarism, indifference and sloth.

But what reward could be greater than to see rising all over the world buildings by men who share the same thoughts, the same ideals! For there occurred a phenomenon unparalleled in the history of art: In spite of the printing press, photography, exhibitions, rapid communications, professional journals, con-gresses, societies and the movies, none of these architects knew about any of the others and they were unaware of the personal experiments of their colleagues—and suddenly a universal style was born spontaneously.

Wright, still unknown yesterday, even by professionals, will soon take his place in the company of the great creative artists. And his work will have an enormous influence, as will that of his colleagues who "see" in the same way. Wright's architecture is human, it is true and will be understood and liked everywhere. Regionalism is dead; with few exceptions, the dwelling of man is the same all over the civilized world, and its beauty must be the same.

Soon fashion will enter the picture. That is unavoidable. Even now one can sense certain tendencies (I won't say "certain formulas"; it would be too harsh) that are taking shape. The phrase is on people's lips: horizontal architecture. In itself, this is a good thing for residences of not many floors; widened openings necessarily result in horizontal parallel lines. But it can be feared that architects without ideas or talent, those who have always copied the past (and what copies!), noticing the popu-larity of these new lines, will hasten to copy as always, mindlessly and illogically. These conscienceless artists seize upon a beautiful idea, deform it and make it so ridiculous that the general public is led to want something else. Works as powerful as Wright's are impossible to plagiarize, but it is already alarming to notice the efforts made by these oppor-tunistic architects to appropriate his ideas and exploit the theft.

All my colleagues know the very sincere respect and admira-tion that I have had for Wright's work, for years now. Therefore I can permit myself a few small criticisms.

We have before us several compositions by the master of undeniable architectural value, but certain roofs seem useless to me. We have often been reproached for systematically doing away with roofs, "those hats of houses." In the first place, a house does not get dressed and can be very beautiful without a hat, as witness the admirable terrace-roofed buildings of Italy and of the eighteenth century in France. Next, the heavy roof (framework and roofing) is not accessible and, without wishing to live on top of one's house, it is very pleasant to be able to make use of that free space prevailing all around. Furthermore, reinforced-concrete construction (at the present time) does not call for a roof. A framework is insufficient to cross the space that must be roofed over. And how much more beautiful is the clean line that finishes off the house!

Having said this, Wright's compositions, as plans and as elevations, may be compared with the great classics. Wright makes his volumes play in space with great mastery, without falling into a pathetic attempt at being picturesque; his compo-sitions reveal a controlled imagination and an attractive rhythm, which produce an impression of cheerfulness and comfort.

Let us make a wish: May his American colleagues, without copying him, immerse themselves in this oeuvre, may they be as fond of him as we are. If some architects in the United States have conceived beautiful buildings, Wright is one of them and he is at the head of the list.

FRANK LLOYD WRIGHT

by Erich Mendelsohn

The following is based on a discussion with Mr. Fiske Kimball, Philadelphia, who has written an article in the June 1925 issue of the *Wasmuth-Monatshefte* about the "Victory of the New Classicism over the Functionalism of the 1890s." [The material in square brackets has been added by the translator, 1992.]

Frank Lloyd Wright's work is controversial.

The party that swears by the permanent validity of historical forms rejects his work.

The party that rejects excessive respect for history swears by his work.

Therefore, to write about Frank Lloyd Wright means coming to terms with both parties.

To regard his work as necessary means remaining objective vis-à-vis both camps.

To love Frank Lloyd Wright means joining one of the camps: deciding in favor of the bold new venture of shaping our own era.

If the attempt to carry through this premise logically with proof and counterproof succeeds, all blame for prejudice, self-defense or egoism is avoided.

Ignoramuses or schoolteachers, both of whom become insecure when confronted by truth, therefore have nothing to fear. For battles of words will not lead to any decision, mirages will afford no clarity. Instead we must think of a procedure that will assure both parties of reaching a common goal.

The opposition party calls [Louis Henri] Sullivan and his school Impressionists.

They mean this in the sense of the Impressionist painting of the middle of last century. At the nadir of its development, this school copied nature by reproducing the instantaneous impression that had been made upon the mediator [i.e., the artist], using any conceivable artistic means, and made the esthetic value of the picture dependent on the degree of faithfulness to nature that had been achieved.

This reproach is valid for the Sullivan of the 1893 World's [Columbian] Exposition in Chicago. For his Transportation Building is only superficially new, in its ornament and detail.

The fact is that, whereas the imitation of nature in Impressionist painting is the decisive factor in the structure of the whole picture, in architecture—as an ornament or a constructed shape—it remains merely two-dimensional trimming and has nothing to do with the truly architectonic element, the three-dimensionality of the space.

Therefore, despite their fundamentally different practical purposes [Charles B.] Atwood's Palace of Fine Arts at the same fair and Sullivan's Transportation Building are in no way different in their constructional principles, but merely in the idiomatic application of ornament.

The thought and the action are the same, both are purely decorative showpieces; only the specific words and gestures are different.

A column remains a column whether it is adorned with pseudo-Greek or with pseudo-Roman foliage, whether it supports an architrave, as a column strictly speaking, or supports a Roman-style arch, in the guise of a pillar. A theatrical performance remains a theatrical performance even when it attempts to pass as living reality.

Only in this sense, therefore, is there any justification in the distinction, "Sullivan's work is naturalistic, Atwood's is abstractly beautiful." But it does not get to the essence of architecture.

Sullivan's Transportation Building should much rather be understood as the first step in his development, perhaps the beginning of every new insight.

For a weakling is seduced into escape by dissatisfaction with everyday, obsolete forms, but it stimulates the courageous man to experiment. Dissatisfaction alone, however, never has the strength to create new foundations. At the outside—as later in Vienna—it leads to a "secession."

Therefore the path of Impressionism was wrong. But by its nature it did not absolutely need to be wrong.

For, upon more mature reflection, the very knowledge of natural processes could have led not to imitation of nature, but to abstraction; that is, acquaintance with the organic and functional laws of nature could have led to the knowledge of the basic elements of a work of art—in painting, color harmony and proportion; in architecture, constructional principles and planning. The second phase of Sullivan's life turns away from this incorrect path of imitating nature and from the purely formal novelties of the Secession.

Here, the opposition party simultaneously calls Sullivan a realist, explaining his realism—again, still on the basis of Impressionism—as the imitation of natural models.

But the theory that architecture, too—that product begotten by the brain of man through thought and vision—ought to judge its own essence by the phenomena of organic nature, leads to the false position of quite superficially and playfully borrowing only lines—thus, only forms—from the constructional conditions of organic life.

And while Europe hastened blindly down this false path—out of weariness with handed-down formalism and not from a lack of new building tasks—while it went into a delirium over Art Nouveau and quickly wore itself out in a linear frenzy, Sullivan many years earlier had admired nature's organizational model. Admired its consequentiality, the way all "organisms" are composed of main and subordinate elements, the meshing of their individual parts—in other words, the absoluteness of their regularity, not the accidental phenomena of their "organs."

And so Sullivan's Guaranty [now Prudential] Building in Buffalo of 1896 [1894–95] refutes the opposition party when that party generalizes its Impressionist "organic theory" and applies it to his work. The Guaranty Building is, as [Fiske] Kimball himself admits, "simple, crystalline, all of a piece"; that is, it is absolute, organic and free of all fortuitousness. In its feeling, to be sure, it is still exaggerated. The newly discovered building material, iron, whose true stress-and-strain possibilities had at that time not yet been thoroughly thought out, overloaded his imagination.

The greater capabilities of the material allowed a hitherto unknown expansion of the dimensions.

Both, the material and the dimensions, led him astray into a dithyramb of verticality.

But iron construction and verticality are by no means necessarily reciprocal. To the present day the construction pattern of skyscrapers is framework. This remains a framework—that is, a lattice—whether it is built of wood, as in the past, or of iron, as it is today. This pattern signified the all but total equality of verticals and horizontals.

But this exaggeration of the vertical dimension, as well as the continuous banding [?],* in the best works of [Joseph Maria] Olbrich and [Henry] van de Velde, appear here as the harbinger of future functional possibilities. It is thus more of a presentiment than a true rebirth.

What still manifests itself in Sullivan's work as a reaction of reason against the irrationality of formalistic ornament is not a "functional vogue," but the logical result of the totality of natural phenomena.

For once upon a time—when first created—the Greek building pattern was also functional—in other words, completely realistic in that sense.

To deny this fact is to disavow altogether the history of the development of continuous, monolithic cultures—the history of styles. It is to deny that the Egyptian hypostyle halls owe part of their origin to the desert and to granite; the Greek porticoes, to the fragrance of the Mediterranean and to marble; the syncopated pilaster arrangements of northern Europe, to the changeable weather and to brick.

Thus the Sullivan of the second period, like everyone in transitional eras, stands between different styles.

In the exaggeration of his realism he cannot fully refute the opposition party's reproach, which it derives from its Impressionist interpretation. But only in this romantic exaggeration.

Fundamentally, his realism has already made the transition to constructivism; that is, it has begun to transfer rationally the constructive, growth-orienting elements of organisms to the constructive elements of architecture, and instead of producing a visible interplay of lines, has made the skeleton of the building tangible.

Therewith Sullivan's career accomplishes the historic leap from Impressionist disintegration to the restabilization of the laws of construction.

Thus Sullivan is "the last great leader of the past," but at the same time a precursor of modernity.

To describe this modernity with precision at this time, or at least to pinpoint the exact spot it has reached on its growth curve, is impossible.

We still do not know the top speed that can be attained.

But the revolutionary play of outward and inward thrusts characteristic of iron and reinforced concrete, and the suppleness of auxiliary building materials inherent in every adventurous construction, have freed buildings from the hitherto existing constraints and weightiness. At any rate, the passion with which the two parties combat each other proves that more than a vogue is at stake in this battle. Both sides are fighting over the elemental principles they cannot live without.

But elemental principles are what everyone has in common.

Here the goal becomes visible; only the viewpoints are different.

---

*The corresponding German word is unusual and may very well contain a typographic error; perhaps the reference is to such features as the bands of windows in Olbrich's 1907 Hochzeitsturm in Darmstadt.

Looking backward: a fettered and timorous mind.
Looking forward: a free and hopeful mind.

The classicists seek after form as the primary consideration. This represents a detour on the path to the elemental, inasmuch as the quest for elements of form is to a certain extent a problem in intellectual computation, as the final result of a series of formulas. The result will be correct if the presuppositions are true.

A convenient path, unadventurous and behind the times.

But we seek after the elements themselves, attaining the forms only afterward, as a logical result.

That is the path of intuition, of bold seeing, of free thinking or, if you will, of experiment. As such, it is not without its dangers. For it is difficult to verify and it is often obstructed by the lagging behind of technical possibilities. Then, too, it often goes astray in its means, because it only sees the goal without calculating the path.

Both paths are inconceivable without a tradition.

Tradition never comes to an end. Every production is a child of its era, conditioned by its era.

Era follows upon era.

But there are obstacles that disturb the usual sequence of developments.

In such cases it is proper to seek a new path.

Seen in this way, both paths are justified.

But the followers of the first path cannot in the long run escape the overpowering force of the new group, which, despite untold effort and frequent defeat, attains its goal in a permanently rejuvenated ascension.

The followers of the second path cannot live in constant experimentation but must ultimately acquiesce in a contented calm so that they can evalute and enjoy their discoveries.

Thus, the first group is compelled to divest itself of its historical form and accept the nakedness of novelty; the second group is born naked.

Then both groups perceive that they are fundamentally the same. Under the pressure of our life and our time, form and style are created from materials and constructive principles as outgrowths of their own era.

Only from such a standpoint can Frank Lloyd Wright be considered.

His work is squarely planted within our era.

Therefore, his rejection of tradition is a thoroughly positive factor.

His development from this concept proceeds logically in response to organic laws, although naturally not without the inner compulsion to make total use of the new building materials to achieve monumentality.

The organization of his buildings is exemplary, pertinent, free, open, full of motion.

The richness of his form-creating ideas is inexhaustible, the harmony of his colors is enchanting.

A great artist, whom we respect.

A great human being, whom we love.